SELF ESTEEM

You're Better Than You Think

* by *

RAY BURWICK

Tyndale House
Publishers, Inc.
Wheaton, Illinois

Unless otherwise noted, all Scripture
quotations are from *The Living Bible*
© 1971, Tyndale House Publishers,
Wheaton, Illinois. Other Scriptures
quoted are from the *King James
Version* and the *New American
Standard Bible* © 1960, 1962, 1963,
1968, 1971 by the Lockman
Foundation, La Habra, California.

Sixth printing, July 1988
Library of Congress Catalog Card Number 82-73455
ISBN 0-8423-5865-X
Copyright © 1983 by Ray Burwick
Printed in the United States of America

to:

My parents, Oliver and Alida Burwick
of Dickinson, North Dakota.
Thanks for your love, worry,
concern, sweat, tears, care, mistakes,
finances, strengths, weaknesses, support,
instruction, example, and discipline,
all of which have had
a great impact on my life,
helping form the Ray Burwick
of today.

Contents

Acknowledgments

I'm grateful to the hundreds of people who have helped me write this book, some of whom appear on the pages with their permission. Others appear camouflaged in order for me to protect their confidentiality.

My busy fourteen-year-old daughter, Amy, who is so gifted as a creative writer, eked out a bit of time to restructure some of the writing.

My wife and receptionist, Ann, gave much of her godly wisdom to make sure that the biblical truths and principles came through clearly. Linda Sims typed, retyped, and provided much encouragement.

Dr. Jack Taylor kindly gave his ideas for improvement of form and construction. Clarke Stallworth edited effectively.

Tom and Edythe Leupp of Portland, Oregon, may your blessings be so great you will not be able to contain them all. You believed in me as an insecure, stuttering college senior and gave me a job. Because of your unconditional love and encouragement, I liked myself more. I'll always be indebted to you.

Preface

It began more than ten years ago. I devoured success-motivation books, records, and seminars in my quest for doing better, being greater. I wanted to like and accept myself.

I could see that the *positive thinking* approach built positive self-esteem, but it didn't seem to plumb the depths of my insecurity and feelings of inadequacy. This approach seemed at best temporary and shallow.

As I faced scores of clients in my counseling office wrestling with the same problem, I knew I had to seek God for a greater insight. What moved me most was the four years that Ann and I shepherded a beautiful group of adult singles. Divorce had scarred and torn up most of their identities.

For my sake and my family's, for my clients, and for the singles, I began digging into the mine shaft of Scripture. The treasure—the mystery of who I was and who I could become—was hacked out of bedrock.

I read book after book, mining a nugget here and there. I wish I could give credit to all the authors who have helped me in the mining operation.

After hundreds of hours of sifting concepts through the sieve of Scripture, I was left with some final nuggets, gleaming in the bottom of the pan. The singles responded enthusiastically. A Sunday school class of 200 at Briarwood Church liked what I said. And even better was the fact that my family noticed a difference in me. Dad was easier to get along with, he was less rigid, and he was taming his harshness. The mining process was sifting and discarding the coarse impurities of my life that kept positive self-esteem from coming to the surface.

My desire for you is that as you read the following material, you'll discover even more clearly all that God has created you to be.

A REAL OR UNREAL PICTURE

He stood six feet five inches and weighed 285 pounds. His thick stumplike neck was rooted on a base of wide shoulders. Not an ounce of fat could be seen on his muscular body. Jim was the meanest machine in pro football, a rising star. Today he walks the streets of Cleveland—disheveled, dirty, and living from one drug fix to the next.

Bill, a middle-aged executive, sits in my counseling office, bent over, with head in hands, and says, "Ray, I had no idea there was any trouble. One day we are a big happy family. The next day I walk in the door and the furniture is gone. My family is gone. There's a note on the kitchen table that says, 'I'm sorry, dear. We just couldn't take it any longer. We'll call you when we get settled and let you know where we are.'"

Jane, a striking brunette with olive skin, fine features, and shapely figure, tells her counselor about her deep depression, "I'm thirty-two and I'm over the hill. There's nothing left to live for. My beauty is fading."

What do these three people have in common? A distorted self-image. They are looking into a twisted mirror.

Jim's self-worth was based only on what he could do on a football field. He had not developed any other part of his life, and a crippling injury killed his brilliant football career. Drugs were his escape.

Bill, like so many men, got caught up in the cyclone of achievement. Self-worth was based on size of car, money in the bank, and position in the company. Work hours were long and exhausting. No creative time and energy were left for his family. They felt neglected.

Jane's self-worth was measured by her looks. Hours were spent every day in front of the mirror. Vast amounts of money went for beauty aids and clothes. If she got a man's eye, she was successful. In her late teens a haunting fear began to develop: "What will happen to my beauty as I grow older? The age of thirty will be the beginning of the end for me," she thought. She was now past thirty. Muscles were not quite as firm. Wrinkles were showing. Her world was crashing. Depression set in.

Each person carries within himself a mental image of the kind of person he thinks he is. This picture shows him as handsome or ugly, capable or inept. Because people tend to have mistaken ideas about themselves, this self-image is not always accurate and can cause great unhappiness.

Some men and women with a lot of talent and capabilities may be held back by unfounded fears that they have little or no ability. The same is true of a person who sees himself as inadequate, inferior, unlovable, and unpopular. Views such as these may be totally wrong, the result of the twisted mirror, a mistaken self-image.

Sometimes a person is his own worst enemy. What he thinks of himself colors his idea of life. If he thinks he is bad, then life is bad. What we think of ourselves will determine the kind of lives we will live.

Whatever the problem that comes to me in my counseling office, whether it is emotional, mental, physical or social, a twisted idea of self is usually in there messing things up.

One of my responsibilities as a counselor is to help people see who they really are, their strengths and weaknesses and the things which need to be changed about them. As weaknesses surface and we see how we should change, we live better. We can then see the good things about ourselves.

Susan sat on my couch in her drab blue hospital garb, fidgety and wild-eyed, though heavily sedated. "Why are we together?" I asked.

"My doctor thought I needed counseling. Three years on medication hasn't taken care of my problems," she related.

When I asked her what her problems were, she painfully, erratically related, "I can't stand noise, I feel like the top of my head is about to blow off. I sometimes feel detached from my brain. I shake a lot, I won't go anywhere for fear of people. I can't stand elevators, heights, or people touching my head. I go to pieces when I have my hair done or the doctor examines my ears. I can't sleep." Then she named three different medications she was taking, and added, "Nothing seems to help."

The temperament analysis profile indicated that Susan had a terribly distorted self-image and had buried much hurt and resentment deep within herself. That first counseling session unfolded some interesting background information—a father who worked, drank, watched TV, divorced his wife when Susan was a teenager, and who became a wandering religious fanatic. Her mother worked outside of the home, was detached, took everything out on the children, hitting them with a dog collar and often yelling how she hated their guts.

"Mom would always fix my hair on Saturdays. She'd tell me I wasn't pretty, would yank on my hair, actually pulling it out by the roots, and slap my face. But even worse, she would flirt with my boyfriends and later even tried to have an affair with my husband." Other rejections surfaced, including an unfaithful, tyrannical husband.

Suppose you were the counselor. Where would you begin?

I asked Susan to go back to her hospital room and write down all the hurts, wrongs, and resentments she could think of. The following day she returned with an even more thorough exposure of thirty years of pain.

She said her ride in the elevator to my office was the best in a long time—no fear. I touched her hair and ears and she didn't cringe. Just knowing what was going on inside of her was beginning to free her from some of the mental handcuffs.

We kept talking. She saw that she needed to be honest with her feelings and attitudes and overcome any negative emotion.

We set about building her self-esteem. Within six weeks there was no more shaking. She had her hair done with no anxiety. Phobias had disappeared. She even applied for and got an excellent job. Depression lifted like a black cloud.

Susan is an exceptional case. What changed the life of a pretty, thirty-year-old mother of two is what can happen to others as they understand the cause and cure for low self-esteem.

ONE

HOW DO I KNOW WHAT'S TRUE?

"How much am I bid for this old violin? Ten dollars... ten dollars and a quarter... who'll give me eleven?"

Buyers stand before the auctioneer, evaluating the wares. A value is placed on each item. That's what *esteem* means.

We evaluate ourselves in the same manner. Positive self-esteem is a realistic appraisal of self, and when we look at ourselves this way, we can see we are like other people. Pride is an unrealistic appraisal of self. We think we are better than others. Low self-esteem is an unrealistic appraisal of self. We think we are not as good as others. And these two things—pride and low self-esteem—stifle God's best for us.

We are probably born with a neutral self-image, neither positive nor negative. The newborn is thrust from its warm, comfortable uterine home into the strange world of the delivery room, with its bright lights and giants scurrying around. Picture the scene. As wet, prunelike newborns, we enter this world of clothed giants. It's a chilly, air-conditioned room with bright lights. We are held up in the air, naked, for inspection and the spank. All eyes are focusing on our nakedness. Our first exposure to humanity is an inspection of our bodies by total strangers.

"It's a boy!" "It's a girl!" And sometimes mom and dad didn't want that brand. Then we are placed in a machine. We are wired with diodes and transistors. Lights expose our nakedness. There we lie for all to see. Now wouldn't that cause anybody a little bit of self-consciousness?

One's picture of himself, actually a cluster of attitudes about self, develops during childhood. Feelings of inferiority or superiority are increased by attitudes of parents, by close relatives, and by friends. One's image of oneself is basically determined by relationships with other people. What we think others are thinking of us determines what we think of ourselves.

Memories, both good and bad, also form self-image. On the one hand, a child's inferiority is constantly pushed on him. "Big people (adults) do what they want to do, go where they want to go. We can't walk; we can't run. We can't touch the TV knob, especially when dad is watching a bunch of big men throwing a ball around. We can't reach the door knob. We usually have to yell to get help in whatever we do or want." Feelings of inferiority and weakness grow.

Along with this, if a child is reared in a cold and hostile family atmosphere, he is likely to grow up believing he is not worth caring about. He thinks he deserves hostility and coldness.

CAUSES OF POOR SELF-ESTEEM

Children who are constantly made fun of or criticized by their parents grow up convinced that they are inferior. Other things parents can do to make sure their children feel inferior are harshness, perfectionism, overprotectiveness, rigidity, controlling, leniency, conditional love, cruel remarks, and absence. Most of these are self-explanatory, but two need talking about.

Overprotectiveness. This is usually a mother's trait. I counseled with Alice, an intelligent young woman, a college graduate, beautiful, a great athlete and musician. Yet she is withdrawing from reality. As I later talked to Alice's mother, I found that she prepares the bed for her twenty-four-year-old daughter each night, rolls back the blankets, lays her nightie out for her, and runs her bath water in the morning. All decision making has been taken over by the mother. This overprotective mother has made Alice feel inadequate. "I guess I just can't do things. Mother has to do everything for me." Alice is withdrawing from reality.

Leniency. So often children see leniency as rejection. "My parents don't really care enough to discipline me." Feelings of rejection and inferiority mount.

Absence. Parents rush to fulfill needs, and send their children to day-care centers and baby-sitters. Parents are gone much of the time, involved in a lot of social events, church activities, business, and other activities. Children pick up the bits and pieces of parents' time and often it is not enough. Some surveys show fathers spend an average of thirty-seven seconds a day with their preschool children. Even when home, TV and the sports page take over the parents' attention. A child begins to feel, "I guess I'm not good enough for mom and dad even to want to spend any time with me."

These rejections give the child a sense of living in a crazy mirror carnival sideshow. One mirror shows him fat and squatty, another tall and skinny. Because he lives with these distorted rejection mirrors day after day, the image of himself is warped and becomes more so as the years pass.

Though inferiority feelings may grow within a child, the child is terribly and completely self-centered and selfish. To himself, he is the most important thing in the world. Having a strong will to control and dominate others, and lacking experience of life, he develops feelings of superiority.

My daughters have baby-sat for a two-year-old who is given free rein with everything. He can go to bed when he chooses. He can eat what and when he chooses—no restrictions. Think of the shock that boy is going to have when he gets out of the home and begins to face some realities of school, of life. Will he be able to manage it?

Feelings and attitudes of superiority, which is actually compensated inferiority, soon bring rejection from playmates, which leads to more feelings of inferiority.

Personal handicaps. Physical deformity, a crippled limb, a speech defect, a divorced home, living in the ghetto are all personal handicaps. The child compares himself with others. "I don't measure up. I don't talk as well as others. I can't walk as well as others. My clothes are not quite as nice as others. I live on the other side of the tracks."

Feelings of inferiority and worthlessness grow, which leads to guilt, self-hate, self-condemnation, and hostility. The child settles for a job half done, or he expects to fail. And his positive self-esteem is destroyed.

Other Signs of Inferiority. I never thought I had an inferiority problem. I was a successful basketball coach, an excellent athlete and musician. My lovely family was developing nicely. But at the age of thirty-two, I faced some tremendous upheaval in my marriage and career, which created an awareness of a gigantic amount of insecurity. Possibly if I had known about self-esteem dynamics earlier, I could have prevented a great deal of pain.

Some of the other traits which might be signs of inferiority are:

1. A pattern of mediocrity—just getting by.
2. Failure—"Everything I do fails."
3. Inability to express feelings, most often a male characteristic.
4. Lack of self-discipline.
5. Deep introspection.
6. Irresponsibility, worry, doubt, fear, pride, jealousy, indecisiveness, clinging to others, blaming others.

A lawyer sat in my office. By the world's standards he had every reason to have a positive self-esteem. He was wealthy, successful in his practice and investments, tall, handsome, and intelligent. You name it, he had it, except peace of mind. Frank had gone through two marriages. He was alienated from his children. Sleep came hard to him. Indigestion was a constant companion.

As we talked I saw that Frank felt good about what he did, but not good about who he was. So often a person feels good about what he *does* (the successful person), but very often not good about *who* he is.

His childhood was marked by achievement-oriented parents—always gone, working or serving the community and the church. The only attention he got was through some great performance, such as straight A's in school or a record-breaking athletic accomplishment. All of his life Frank set goals for himself. "Set your sights high. Do your best. Be the best," he always believed.

There is nothing wrong with this philosophy except that Frank had neglected building relationships. He was a workaholic. His self-esteem was based upon performance. Children and two wives had been neglected too long and had left. Frank, not feeling good about himself (inferiority), escaped through the world of work. He was like a prisoner trying to escape from jail.

OTHER WAYS TO ESCAPE

Fantasy world. One of the common complaints from women in my counseling practice is that their husbands come home tired, take a quick shower, grab something to eat, and flop down in front of the TV. Obviously, men get tired working, but so often television is an escape machine. Many men dislike intimate family communication. They feel inadequate to handle the unpleasantness of interpersonal relationships. Men's insecurity and feelings of inferiority find a neat escape route through TV, sports, work, clubs, church, drugs, alcohol, daydreaming, and other diverse activities.

Going back to the cradle is probably the most severe escape mechanism. I worked with an intelligent young businessman who had a very overprotective mother who never let him make decisions. His father always took his hard knocks for him. He would lose money in business and his father would step in and pay off bills. Joe had not developed the ability to be responsible.

One day he was missing. His wife looked all over for him. Late afternoon she found him in a back room of their business office, curled in the fetal position, sucking his thumb.

Joe was a Christian but he was unable to face the tremendous amount of pressure going on, not only in the business but within himself. Joe's thinking went something like this: "I just don't feel capable to handle all that is going on. I'll crawl off in the corner and become a baby again. Someone else will have to take care of me and handle the pressure."

Masking is another escape. The bully, the tyrant, the bluffer hide themselves from themselves and others, afraid that a flaw will surface. The bluffer poses as a very dynamic person, dramatizing how great he is. But he must run from one job to the next, lest failure catch up and expose him for who he really is.

The person who overcompensates, like the great athlete, is

often one involved in an escape mechanism. "World, notice me, tell me I'm OK." Because the person is not resolving personal insecurities, there is a tremendous drive to be successful. Are all great athletes over-compensators? No, but many are.

Projection. Looking down at others is often seen in racial prejudice. "I don't feel good about myself, so I look down at another race or another religion. I'm better than they are."

Rationalization. "I could have done that, but. . . ." I'm counseling a man in his fifties, who has never been married. He develops a dating relationship. When it becomes serious he panics. But instead of admitting his fears and inadequacies, he sees a flaw in the woman. "Her eyes are not slanted right. I can't accept her." So he drops her.

Then he begins to build another relationship. The relationship becomes close and intimacy begins. All of a sudden he notices her nose is out of line a bit.

Peter refuses to see through his defense mechanism even when I gently confront him with, "Hey, you're wrapped up in a mess of inferiority that says, 'I could never handle the responsibilities of being married, and instead of facing that fact, I'll find some little flaw in the lady's face.' "

The final escape is suicide, which is the second leading cause of death among young people. "I just don't want to face what is going on within me, so I'll take my life."

Often, suicide is the ultimate "get-even" method. When I gently confront a client of mine now with something she doesn't like to hear, instead of telling me how angry she is with me, she says, "I'll slash my wrists."

Cases of suicide in children are rare. Their insecurity is often seen in the shy, quiet, withdrawn child or the superactive, aggressive child. Both of these extremes are inferiorities expressing themselves through withdrawal or aggressive compensation.

If they aren't dealt with, teenage and adult years continue with further withdrawal or rebellion. Rebellion can take the form of lashing out, lashing in (emotional-mental problems), and often sexual promiscuity.

Men will say, "I don't feel good about myself, so the more notches I get on my belt the more I feel like a man."

Women say, "I don't feel very good about myself. The only way I'm going to get a man is to go to bed with him." Inferiority leads to all kinds of problems.

So far, the tone of this book has been a "downer." But we need to know the kinds of wounds that can come from running oneself down, causing negative self-esteem. So many of us won't think about it until we "crash and burn." And that shouldn't happen to anyone of us.

PERSONAL APPLICATION

How do we know if we have a distorted self-image? To some of us, that is a crazy question. Our poor self-image is clearly visible for all to see.

However, many have hidden their inferiority feelings so well that they are not even aware of poor self-esteem, yet live with the destructive elements of it.

There is no comprehensive self-esteem evaluation. However, if the following statements are answered honestly we may have a better understanding of ourselves and the material in this book will then have more meaning.

An *agree* response to any statement can be a sign of less than perfect self-esteem. Many *agree* or *agree strongly* responses indicate that the book will have great value to us in our personal growth process.

For best results, we may have one of our closest friends evaluate us also. We should compare the results of his/her evaluation with our own for greater understanding of ourselves.

Self-Esteem Evaluation

	STRONGLY AGREE	SLIGHTLY AGREE	DISAGREE
1. When faced with a difficult task, I either do not try at all or give up easily.	☐	☐	☐
2. People unjustly walk all over me.	☐	☐	☐
3. I am careful never to depend on others.	☐	☐	☐
4. I often find myself clinging to another person.	☐	☐	☐
5. I rarely discuss my deepest thoughts with anyone.	☐	☐	☐
6. I constantly seek companionship.	☐	☐	☐
7. I seek to be alone rather than participate socially.	☐	☐	☐
8. I tend to put myself down and exaggerate the importance of others.	☐	☐	☐
9. I am shy and feel nervous when with others.	☐	☐	☐
10. It makes me angry when people compare me to others who are doing better than myself.	☐	☐	☐
11. I usually blame others for my problems.	☐	☐	☐
12. I fear rejection and will do most anything to obtain approval.	☐	☐	☐
13. I dwell on the unfavorable remarks and criticisms made by others.	☐	☐	☐
14. I try to attract attention by any method that seems likely to succeed.	☐	☐	☐
15. I try to govern others.	☐	☐	☐

STRONGLY AGREE · SLIGHTLY AGREE · DISAGREE

16. I often try to get even with people who wrong me. ☐☐☐

17. I feel satisfaction from ill news about another, even a public figure whom I do not know. ☐☐☐

18. I need a sense of accomplishment (doing something) at all times. ☐☐☐

19. I play second fiddle too much, always a follower and never a leader, even permitting myself to be led against my will and better judgment. ☐☐☐

20. I can't accept praise without some embarrassment. ☐☐☐

21. I'm easily jealous. ☐☐☐

22. I often boast about myself. ☐☐☐

23. I am a very competitive person and must always win. I'll even take advantage of others to win. ☐☐☐

24. I find it difficult to make decisions. ☐☐☐

25. I am often loud and boisterous. ☐☐☐

26. I fear being different. ☐☐☐

27. If I fail to get recognition, I pout. ☐☐☐

28. I am a perfectionist and often see myself as more capable than others. ☐☐☐

29. I'm very selfish. ☐☐☐

	STRONGLY AGREE	SLIGHTLY AGREE	DISAGREE
30. When listening to another, I find myself thinking about what I'll say when I get a chance.	☐	☐	☐
31. I don't compliment others.	☐	☐	☐
32. God is not interested in my everyday life.	☐	☐	☐
33. I enjoy correcting the mistakes of others.	☐	☐	☐
34. I enjoy saying things that will embarrass others.	☐	☐	☐
35. I enjoy frequent gossip sessions.	☐	☐	☐
36. I have a difficult time making and keeping friends.	☐	☐	☐
37. Laziness, procrastination, and lack of self-discipline are problems for me.	☐	☐	☐
38. I often compare myself with others.	☐	☐	☐
39. I often fail.	☐	☐	☐
40. I tend to spend much of my time in self-evaluation.	☐	☐	☐

T W O

A DISTORTED IMAGE

The more inferior we feel, the more we look inward. We are quick to look at things around us to see how they will touch us, which opens up a Pandora's box of problems.

One of the resultant problems is *self-absorption*. "I've got to have more self-confidence," one says. The search begins—self-help books, tapes, seminars, learning—so we can think and feel better about ourselves.

There is nothing wrong with seeking a more positive self-esteem, except that self-absorption is often the result. Instead of really knowing ourselves and feeling better about ourselves, we turn ever inward and open ourselves to things which tear down our self-esteem.

Another way insecurity destroys is *performance orientation,* with thoughts such as: "Achieve; do; be the best; be the quickest; to the top." Though we get a lot done, it leads to stomach ulcers, high blood pressure, heart problems, loss of family relationships, and often suicide.

Performance, achievement, and doing well are all important. But the more insecure or inferior we feel, the more important performance becomes. "Hey, look at me, world. Tell me I'm OK."

This emphasis on performance can lead us to hours and days gripped by destructive anxieties, which lower our resistance to disease and push us to many kinds of physical problems. One of my clients tells of her performance-orientation experience this way:

> Perfect—that's what I've tried to be most of my life. As a little girl, I wanted to be pretty. I have a beautiful sister. People turn their heads and look at her when we walk down the street together. I never was jealous of her. I love her dearly, but I saw myself as the ugly duckling of the two. I tried very hard most of my young life to be as my mother said—"pretty is as pretty does." I tried to live up to that and I thought that if I "did pretty," maybe I'd be pretty. I became performance-oriented.

I figured out at an early age that if I did what other people wanted me to do and expected of me, I would be accepted, patted on the head, and loved. I've been an actress in many plays here at the church. It was very easy for me because I had been acting most of my life—acting like somebody else, not acting like Alice.

I didn't know who I really was for many, many years because I kept trying to be what the people I was with wanted me to be, and that's hard work. It was so hard that by the time I became a Christian, twenty years ago, I was relieved to accept Christ's love and his acceptance of me. For a long time those old patterns fell away and I experienced a productive, happy, useful existence. But somehow, the old patterns began to reestablish themselves again and that perfectionist person resurfaced. I kept trying to earn God's love and acceptance, as I had previously tried to earn everybody else's.

I failed. God had to let me fail, because his acceptance is not something that we can ever earn. He's already accepted us—no performance is necessary. But I kept drumming up all this energy to try to be the perfect Christian. I failed.

As I failed, I began to turn my thoughts inward more and more and became terribly self-absorbed. As this happened, I unknowingly began building up anger and resentment toward anybody and everybody. About six months ago I listened to a speaker on the subject of anger. He said, "Now some of you are sitting here saying, 'I'm not angry.' " I just sat there and said, "I'm not angry." He said, "You're just saying, 'I'm hurt.' " I said, "That's me. I'm not angry, I'm hurt."

Then he said something that wiped me out. "Hurt is a blanket to cover up anger." I couldn't avoid that, because I realized it must be true. I had been internalizing this anger toward all the influences in my life and all the people in my life who expected, I thought, this perfect person.

It made me sick and I mean very ill, with a neck problem that caused disks to degenerate, for which I was on anti-inflammatory drugs for three years with muscular pain, depression, and digestive disturbances. I also had an allergy to milk which triggered other problems. Then I began to develop pain in my back, where the kidneys are located. I was going to a kidney specialist who recommended surgery. But I didn't have the time or energy to have surgery.

After that morning session of talking about pent-up anger, I called the speaker the next week and said, "Hey, you put the finger on something and I need some help."

The results of the counseling were amazing. I don't take medication for my neck anymore. I'm not having surgery on my kidney. Depression is gone. I feel a freedom and a wholeness that I haven't known for years and years.

It's akin to being born again. It's very much akin to that freedom and that experience that I had twenty years ago when I first knew the Lord, because really I know him again.

I believe in reality that my position in Christ is real. That has made all the difference in the world in me, spiritually, physically, emotionally, and mentally.

For years I walked with my smiling, Christian look, embarrassed and ashamed to admit that I had problems. My pride kept me in bondage to all my physical ailments. Pride was swallowed. I sought counsel. I'm free! This means everything and I wouldn't trade the problems I've had for anything in the world, because of the help that I have received and the future I'm facing.

The counselor did not have any special gift of healing for this woman. As she began to see who she really was in Christ, symptoms began to go away all by themselves.

Inadequacy feelings lead to a problem called *impression formation*. We live as we see ourselves. Impression formation is typified by one who says, "I see myself a certain way and no matter what you say to me, it doesn't change how I feel about myself."

That's the reason many have a hard time accepting compliments. If I don't feel very good about myself or think very well of myself, all the compliments in the world can't penetrate my misperception. I discount them.

Failure and *mediocrity* are also signs of a poor self-esteem. Picture the baby elephant, chained to a stake. Those first days the little elephant tugs away furiously. The chain doesn't snap. The stake stays in the ground. He keeps pulling, trying to get free. Soon the pattern, the habit, the way of thinking, becomes ingrained. "There's no way I can pull loose from this chain. The stake has held me firmly to the ground and no matter what I do, I can't free myself from it."

Years later we see that elephant of several tons still tied by that little chain and stake. All he would have to do is flick a little leg muscle and the chain would snap or the stake would fly. But he has been programmed: "I can't release myself from that chain."

All the power in the world is within him to do so, but he doesn't. In chain-stake pulling, he has become failure-oriented.

Often we have been so controlled by inferior feelings that we have programmed our minds to think, "I'm just going to have to be satisfied with mediocrity. That's my lot in life."

Another way inferiority hurts is "*slavery.*" "If I don't feel very good about myself, I become a slave to those around me. I'm easily influenced by other people. I need their approval. I'll live any kind of way you want me to live, so I can get your acceptance."

"Slavery" causes a lot of stress. To get relief, we often gobble great amounts of food, drugs, or alcohol. Or we play some hurtful mental game such as self-pity or lust.

In my counseling office I work with a lot of men who say, "You know, Ray, I really have to wrestle with lust." As we begin to talk and to explore backgrounds, I see that rejection plays a part. Natural lust within us is often poisoned by a tremendous desire to be accepted by women because of the mother-rejection in childhood. This may sound weird and probably Freudian. But it has been amazing to see that these men, as they look at a woman lustfully and quickly say, "Lord, you are my acceptance, I don't need that woman's acceptance," the power of lust is weakened.

Sometimes as a result of inferiority feelings, we become *easily threatened*. If we don't think we are adequate, we become easily threatened by any kind of challenge.

One result of feeling threatened is anger, which causes all kinds of hell—emotional, mental, physical, social, spiritual. See the author's book, *Anger: Defusing the Bomb* (Wheaton: Tyndale House Publishers, 1981).

Inferiority also leads to a *faulty relationship with God*. If I don't feel or think very well of myself, I ask, "Who made me?" "God made me, and if he made me like this, how can I trust him?" Or, "I'm so bad, I'm not good enough to get his acceptance, his approval, his blessing." False guilt is the result.

Inferior feelings can lead to *conceit*. Some of the most proud, cocky people we face are those who don't feel very good about themselves. They mask it with conceit. "Be not wise in thine own eyes: fear the Lord, and depart from evil" (Proverbs 3:7, KJV). "Woe to them that are wise in their own eyes, and prudent in their own sight!" (Isaiah 5:21, KJV). "If anyone thinks he knows all the answers, he is just showing his ignorance" (1 Corinthians 8:2). Conceit gets us into trouble.

In the Alcoholics Anonymous program, a typical pattern for some of those with a problem is that they go to AA, aware that there is a drinking problem. They get involved and don't drink for a week, a month, three months, and suddenly they become overly confident. The foggy mind is clearing. They feel better. At this point there is sometimes a fall. "I can handle just one drink. I believe those were problems of the past." Conceit leads to one drink which sends them to the pits again. They must admit that they can't handle even one drink.

As I study Scripture, I always look for counseling concepts, and probably the most classic example of conceit in Scripture is recorded in Daniel:

> Twelve months later, as the king [Nebuchadnezzar] was walking on the roof of the royal palace of Babylon, he said, "Is not this the great Babylon I have built as the residence by my mighty power and for the glory of my majesty?" The words were still on his lips when a voice came from heaven, "This is what is decreed for you, King Nebuchadnezzar. Your royal authority has been taken from you. You will be driven away from the people and live with the wild animals; you will eat grass like cattle. Seven years will pass by for you until you acknowledge that the Most High is sovereign over the kingdoms of men and gives them to anyone he wishes." Immediately what was said about Nebuchadnezzar was fulfilled. He was driven away from his people and ate grass like cattle. His body was drenched with the dew of heaven until his hair grew like the feathers of an eagle and his nails like the claws of a bird. At the end of the seven years, I, Nebuchadnezzar, raised my eyes toward heaven and my sanity was restored.

Notice the parallel. In the first verse, he was looking *down* at all he had accomplished. Seven years later he was looking *up*, saying, "In me, (that is in my flesh, in my self-centeredness) is no good thing. Then I praised the Lord Most High. I honored and glorified him who lives forever." What a change in attitude!

Conceit can hurt us. A poor self-image can destroy us. However, negative self-perception can also help us, as we shall see.

T H R E E

CAN I KNOW THE REAL ME?

The best thing that could happen to some people might be to struggle with a poor self-image. Charles R. Solomon in his book, *Ins and Out of Rejection* (Denver: Heritage House, 1976) says that the well-adjusted Christian, walking in the power of self, has a most devastating problem because he usually doesn't realize that he has a problem. His religious flesh tends toward self-righteousness and pride.

However, Christians with the most severe hang-ups are most ready to face their need and receive their resources from Christ. They are forced to rely completely on the Lord, as Paul described: "Glory be to God who by his mighty power at work within us is able to do far more than we would ever dare to ask or even dream of—infinitely beyond our highest prayers, desires, thoughts, or hopes" (Ephesians 3:20).

God has planned for us greater things than we can even dream about. But we can't experience them until we see how in our self-centered power there is no way we can experience what God has in store for us. In fact, we fall flat on our faces if we really try to conjure up enough strength to experience what God has in mind for us.

Paul described the ideal Christian life in Romans 6. In Romans 7 he went on to say that it is impossible to live. In Romans 8 he described how to experience it through the power of the Holy Spirit at work within us.

This awareness of our inadequacy must come through some personal trauma—divorce, a business reversal, physical problems—or through an awareness that there is no way we can live Matthew 5, 6, and 7 (love your enemies, do good to those who hate you, turn the other cheek, if a man wants your coat give him your shirt, too).

Paul described the value of inadequacy:

Each time he said, "No. But I am with you; that is all you need. My power shows up best in weak people." Now I am glad to boast about how

weak I am; I am glad to be a living demonstration of Christ's power. . . .
Since I know it is all for Christ's good, I am happy about "the thorn,"
and about insults and hardships, persecutions and difficulties; for when
I am weak, then I am strong—the less I have, the more I depend on
him (2 Corinthians 12:9, 10).

In John 15, Jesus said, "Without me you can do nothing." I'm not
really sure what that means. I realize that I can't take one step
here without God, because he could wipe me out before I take
that step. That might be the interpretation of the verse; or, it
might be, "Without me you can do nothing in comparison to what
you do with me."

Until I was twenty-eight years old, stuttering dominated my
life. As a young boy I was raised by my mother who stuttered.
We lived way out in the "sticks" of North Dakota, where bath-
rooms were seventy-five feet downwind. Population in that area
was sparse. Dad worked long days in the field. Mom and I were
together most of the time. I learned to speak like her and, not
knowing any better, she would slap me when I stuttered because
she thought I was mocking her. This created more tension and
caused more stuttering. The pain and embarrassment were hor-
rendous. I have even thrown my jaw out of place trying to get a
word out.

Speech therapy was initiated when I was a youngster. I learned
that I was not alone. Two and a half million Americans stutter,
four times as many men as women. Famous people such as Sir
Isaac Newton, Winston Churchill, W. Somerset Maugham, and
Moses were stutterers.

There were a lot of theories. Hippocrates believed a dry tongue
caused stuttering. A "refrigerated tongue" was seventeenth-cen-
tury philosopher Francis Bacon's diagnosis. Hot wine was the
remedy. A Russian physician in the 1800s sliced a stutterer's
tongue down to size because stuttering was caused by a tongue
too large. Fortunately, I still have my tongue intact. But I tried
almost everything else.

One therapist had me slow my speech down and slur into

words. Another suggested I move my finger like a metronome and speak in rhythm. I've knocked on doors of total strangers to ask the time of day and tell them I stuttered.

I've tried Demosthenes' "pebbles in the mouth" approach, hypnosis, and drug therapy (to relax). I've had the world's best-known faith healer pray for me. Nothing worked permanently.

Some people said, "Ray, I hope you realize that you just don't have enough faith. If you would pray and expect God to heal you of your stuttering, you wouldn't stutter anymore." So I'd get my knee pads on and pray hour after hour, "Lord, heal me; I believe you can heal me," and I'd get up stuttering more. That was frustrating.

Then others would say, "Ray, I hope you never stop stuttering. It's such an inspiration to me to hear you up there spitting and sputtering. That encourages me to want to share also." So there was the frustration of not even knowing how to pray.

When I was twenty-eight years old, I was on a TV basketball show in Salt Lake City. We were playing the University of Utah that night and taping a pregame interview. I stuttered so much that the show was cancelled. Stuttering was embarrassing, painful, and frustrating. But now I'm thankful for it, because at the age of twenty-eight, I began to see that there were causes for stuttering. God didn't want to heal my symptom. He wanted to remove the causes.

Feelings of inadequacy and unresolved anger surfaced as the causes. I began to work on it. But I became aware of something more important. Jesus speaking: "Ray, where you're weak, I can become strong. I can do much more through you than you can do in the power of your own self, for my power shows up best in weak people."

"Lord, thank you for my insecurity and my feeling of inadequacy," I prayed. Before every speaking opportunity I have to say, "Lord, I can't do it. I'll have to take bath towels so that the people closest to me can wipe off after I get through spitting and sputtering all over them. Lord, speak through me. Take my weakness. Be my strength."

We can really get excited about insecurity and inadequacy. Poor self-image can build us up. We can enter any situation, no matter how threatening, and remind ourselves that God's power shows up best in our weakness. Think of it! The Creator of this whole universe is alive and speaking through us! Fantastic!

Some may call this a delusion of grandeur. I like to see it as a Christian tapping into the supernatural power available to him.

Not long ago, I spoke to a large gathering of doctors and their wives. My insecurity reared its ugly head. "Who do you think you are, teaching such a knowledgeable group as this? You're not as intelligent as they are. What if you start stuttering? What will they think?"

On and on played in my mind the forty-year-old tape that said, "You're inadequate."

How absolutely thrilling it was to insert and play a "new identity" tape: "You're right. Without Christ I can do nothing. I am inadequate to the task. But, I've done my homework. I'm prepared. And I claim the same promise God gave to Moses."

> But Moses pleaded, "O Lord, I'm just not a good speaker. I never have been, and I'm not now, even after you have spoken to me, for I have a speech impediment." "Who makes mouths?" Jehovah asked him. "Isn't it I, the Lord? Who makes man so that he can speak or not speak, see or not see, hear or not hear? Now go ahead and do as I tell you, for I will help you to speak well, and I will tell you what to say" (Exodus 4:10-12).

The medical seminar was a success.

PERSONAL APPLICATION

Material such as this won't do the reader much good unless it is personalized. Each of us should ask, "How do I like myself? What is my 'stuttering'?" Perhaps our problem is a deformed body, or a different sort of personality, or some overwhelming weakness. Possibly we have come through some very hurtful experience that wiped out the underpinnings of our self-confidence —divorce, bankruptcy, or some other kind of failure.

What is our response? Is it making us better or bitter? Is it causing our feelings about ourselves to become more and more negative? Or is it driving us deep into a close relationship with God from whom we are receiving a taste of supernatural living?

How is this supernatural living achieved? How do we change the twisted mirror image—the negative self-perception to positive self-esteem? Read on; there's help ahead.

FOUR

SEEKING THE REAL ME

Several years ago God was declared dead. The search for the only true deity, self, began and a merry chase it has been for over a hundred years. Almost the whole of modern psychology revolves around it. As Calvin Linton graphically described it, one layer after another of the "man onion" has been peeled in search of the innermost seed, the divine essence, the *me* who is God. For a long time it has been as much fun as opening Christmas presents. There seems to be no end to the box within boxes.

Now, however, the fear seems to be growing that the last wrapping has been removed, the last layer peeled, and there is nothing inside. A sort of psychological black hole of the astronomer, the soundless scream of Hitler's gas baths. The man god, at last self-known, curls into a fetal position and waits... for nothing.

DEVELOPING THE PHYSICAL SELF

Man, self-known, has "found" himself through one of four avenues: (1) the physical self; (2) relationships; (3) performance; and (4) status. Man endeavors to build self-esteem through development of the physical self.

Appearance. It is said that the cosmetics industry is one of the few industries that does not suffer during a recession. Much effort is spent on looking and smelling right by using the right cosmetics. Much time is spent with hair. If conservative clothes are in, nothing flashy is worn.

One of our daughters, when eleven years old, was a tall five feet seven inches and wore size 9 or 10 shoes. Most of her classmates were a foot shorter. She would slink down the halls, trying hard to be unnoticed. Stooped shoulders were her trademark. Insecurity reigned supreme until she took a modeling course.

She did well in the course, got a modeling job one weekend, and was in a beauty contest, where she won a couple of trophies. Now guess how tall she stands. Five feet nine and rising!

But there can be a problem. She felt much better about herself. But the natural tendency in this "remedy" for poor self-esteem is to focus on outward beauty. Makeup must be exact, hair done perfectly, clothes the appropriate style. Many are the girls who won't go out of the house without makeup on.

Let's face reality. As we approach thirty, wrinkles set in and muscles sag. Clothes go out of style, or there's a business reversal and there's no money to buy new clothes. If our self-esteem is based on outward appearance only, we're setting ourselves up for trouble.

There is nothing wrong with looking better. We should look good. We, as Christians, are children of God—special, unique—not better than anyone else, not worse than anyone else, but great. We should appear appropriately. But if our identity is determined by our outward appearance, it is so easy to get happy when people compliment us, or if they ignore us, to fold up entirely.

The *intellect*. There is a friend of mine, a brilliant doctor, from the Northwest, who built an identity upon his mental capacity. He was doing very well until he met two other physicians who were more intelligent than himself. In only a few days he was in deep depression. The psychiatrist recommended shock treatment as the only way out. What would shock treatments do to a medical doctor? "It could wipe out my medical expertise!" he said. Fortunately, we were able to tap the cause of depression, build a positive self-esteem, and resolve it without the shock therapy.

Developing our mental capacities does build positive self-esteem, but if our identity is based on being the smartest, we're heading for a letdown. Besides, the wiser we are the more we know that the difference between what the most and least learned people know is trivial compared to all that is unknown!

Power of Positive Thinking. We are what we think. "As [a man] thinketh in his heart, so is he," the Bible says. If we think negatively, we act negatively. We are just scratching the surface in our knowledge of what the human mind can do.

A doctor friend of mine stated, "I had exhausted all medical remedies for a cancer patient. Nothing worked; he was getting worse. The patient then started a daily mental exercise: 'Tumor in the lung, you're getting smaller and smaller.' The cancerous tumor dissipated and he has no sign of cancer." A Texas physician uses mental visualization in all cancer treatment.

Power of positive thinking—I believe in it. It's biblical. But I tried that as the way of building my self-esteem and it didn't work. I had my $300 case of positive thinking records. I would play them every morning and go out to lick the world. Two minutes later, something would make me angry or threaten me and I was wiped out. Positive thinking is good. We need to think positively, but it doesn't touch the deep insecurities and the deep inadequacies that some of us pack around.

Looking good, developing our minds, thinking positively, eating properly, involvement in a consistent exercise program, recreation, or skin care—all enhance our self-esteem from a physical perspective, but these are only partial answers.

SUMMING UP

There are four ways that we can go to build a positive self-image: (1) the physical self; (2) relationships; (3) performance; and (4) status.

Relationships. Most child development theorists believe that a child literally discovers what kind of person he is and how he feels about himself by the reactions of his parents to him. This is a natural childhood phenomenon. But so often we carry it over into our adult years and try to build self-esteem on how we think others see us.

If someone makes us feel comfortable about ourselves, we feel accepted and worthy. By others' comments and attitudes, we see how they view us. That's nice when they are positive toward us. But if they are not praising us, we feel rejected and hurt. That leads to building walls of protection, withdrawal, and usually a lot of hostility. Unresolved anger causes all kinds of psychosomatic illnesses and social problems.

The final negative reaction to rejection is suicide. I counseled a man recently who showed me a "suicide" bullet. It had a little dent on the firing cap where the firing pin had hit. But the gun didn't fire. My client said, "Ray, I had enough hurt and rejection from people. I got my gun and I prayed, 'Lord hold my hand steady.' " He pulled the trigger but the bullet failed. People had really let him down, he thought.

Positive relationships have to be established. As brothers and sisters in Christ, we do need to be loving each other and building each other up. But if our identity is based upon how we build each other up, sooner or later there will be a problem. We don't always get encouragement and support. We get hurt, which can wipe out our positive identity, if positive relationships are what our identity is based on. For this reason I discourage a steady dating relationship before age sixteen. Most teenagers are not equipped to handle rejection before this age, and some not even later.

Achievement. Achievement is a way to build positive self-image. Newspaper columnist Sidney Harris said, "Young people searching for their real self must learn that the real self is not something that one finds as much as it is something one makes. It is one's daily actions that shape the inner personality far more permanently than any amount of introspection or intellectualization. Performance becomes the source of identity."

Harris's statement has merit, but there is a definite weakness. The champion athlete, the A student, the spotless housekeeper, the "hostess with the mostest," the "perfect" Christian, the outstanding businessman, all feel good about themselves because of their achievement. But what happens if achievement fails? What happens if we bottom out or top out?

I counseled a man recently who had been a multimillionaire. He was later counting pennies. His millions had been wiped out. His self-esteem was in tatters.

Imagine the perfect housewife. All is well at home. Things are running smoothly. All of a sudden she finds out that her husband is having an affair with another woman. What does that do to her self-esteem if it was based totally on being a perfect housewife?

Achievement-oriented self-esteem can have other problems. Tremendous hurts and rejections in childhood could have programmed your computer: "I'm a failure; I'm not good enough; it will never work for me and as much as I try to achieve, to perform, to do well—I know that somewhere along the line, I'm going to fail; I won't be able to maintain that consistent performance."

A voice inside says, "It's not going to last, Burwick. It's not good enough, Burwick."

Performance-based self-esteem always seems to end in failure. Failure shatters a person who seeks to build identity on achievement. The poor loser, the athlete with a terrible temper, is basing self-image on his performance.

Growth of spiritual pride is another weakness of achievement-oriented self-esteem. Often, new Christians get involved so deeply in church that every time the doors open they are there. Bible studies and witnessing—a whole lot of great things are being accomplished, but the result is spiritual pride. "Look at how good I am. See what a busy Christian I am. See how well I'm doing."

James wrote: "What you ought to say is, 'If the Lord wants us to, we shall live and do this or that.' Otherwise you will be bragging about your own plans, and such self-confidence never pleases God" (James 4:15, 16).

Next time you and I are tempted to think too highly of ourselves we need to remember that there are 800 million Chinese who have never heard of us.

My prayer book for July 19, 1976, reads: "God, these inferior feelings are so ugly. Please change me." This came after I had achieved quite a lot. I feel a bit like Paul right now, as he said, "I kind of hate to brag about myself, but I need to tell you these things for these certain reasons" (2 Corinthians 10—11).

In school I was all-state basketball and leading scorer for the state. I was a successful punter in football; won many track ribbons and trophies; was first-chair trumpet with superior ratings in solo competition. I was a sports editor of a daily newspaper at the age of eighteen; was most valuable player at a basketball camp sponsored by some of the Boston Celtics; was one of the leading basketball scorers in the Northwest college and university circuit; and was elected to Outstanding Young Men of America and *Who's Who in American Colleges and Universities*.

I moved directly from college into a college head-basketball coaching position, and while that was going on, I moved houses, had a landscaping service, a janitorial service, and I sold real estate. I had a great coaching record at the college.

We had a nice house, a little cabin cruiser, and a Cadillac. Later I joined American Athletes in Action and played some of the top teams in America. I have originated two different counseling practices; at the age of thirty-eight I began a doctoral program and finished it three years later. I've written a book that is selling very well.

No, I'm not a Rockefeller or a Kennedy. But for an old North Dakota farm boy there has been a smidgin of success.

But even with the success, there was that haunting ghost of "I'm not good enough." I was stuttering more and enjoying it less, even during basketball games.

Time-outs in basketball games are only one minute. One of my challenges as a coach was to know the game officials and make sure they would give me some extra time.

During one time-out, I was stuck on a word and a player said, "Sing it, coach." (Stutterers don't stutter when they sing.)

I was stuttering more, also suffering with a spastic colon, and other psychosomatic problems persisted, which I didn't link with poor self-esteem, even though I considered myself successful.

"Successful people don't have poor self-esteem problems," I told myself. Little did I realize at that point that there was a little guy inside of me crying out to the world, "Notice me, tell me I'm OK."

My source of identity was that neurotic drive to prove to myself and to the world that I was an adequate person. The list of accomplishments meant I was acceptable, right? Wrong!

The achievement gates closed. Basketball coaching ended. Life in the limelight ceased. It seemed that I was in a back desert kind of experience, herding sheep, like Moses in Exodus 2.

Self-esteem based on achievement began to crumble. There was an identity crisis. There was not the ego-building thrill of massive basketball arenas, screaming fans, and scoreboard lights indicating victory. I was sitting behind a desk, quietly working one on one with Christians, trying to help them grow.

What an emotional letdown. I'd often say to my wife, "Ann, I want to be a star."

Men in their 30s and 40s often go through this "male menopause" experience. Achievements and ambition, though never satisfied, do lead to better feelings about ourselves. However, a "top-out" or "take-away" experience can set us up for a crash emotionally.

Status. The last avenue on man's map for building positive self-esteem is status. Status symbols are the kind of car I drive, the career that I have, my house and its location—even marrying into the right family even though there's not the proper love and commitment.

Status symbols have other dimensions, such as name dropping, and mentioning the neat opportunities we have had for Christian witness. "Hey! Notice. I'm an adequate person, am I not?"

How is our self-esteem? Status is a reality, performance is excellent, physical self is strong, relationships are good, but what happens if our security or significance is threatened?

Suppose there is a sickness, or child-raising trauma, or a business reversal, or wrinkles. A divorce or death occurs, or the top-out experience comes. If building positive self-esteem is based totally on our methods that we have just talked about, identity begins to crumble.

This week I counseled a bright, intelligent couple. She had gone through a lot of emotional and mental trauma lately, but is becoming whole and free. He, however, is coming apart. His self-worth had been built on how well he could take care of her and how she needed him. That type of relationship is gone and his identity is destroyed. He had been the picture of confidence and strength and a leader in a big business, but that day he sat in my office and wept like a little boy.

PERSONAL APPLICATION

Man's way of achieving positive self-esteem is built on partial truth.

Let us take a moment for personal evaluation, to score ourselves on a scale of 1 to 10; one being *shabby, never,* or *nothing,* and 10 meaning *always* or *perfect.*

Appearance—Looking as attractive as we can.   _____

Intellect—Reading, studying, developing mental skills.   _____

Positive Thinking—Bringing negative thoughts and words into captivity, exchanging them with positive.   _____

Relationships—Associating with positive, productive, caring people who build us up instead of tearing us down.   _____

Achievement—Laziness or lack of self-discipline, lack of accomplishing tasks and goals, tears down positive self-esteem.   _____

Status—Don't score this item. Status symbols are a false sense of positive identity.

If our score is above 35, great! If not, let us get to work.

This evaluation would be enhanced if we had a close friend or relative score his view of us on each item. We should then compare the two and discuss it with the other person. We often have blind spots. Others can help us see ourselves better if we encourage them to do so.

Man's way of building positive self-esteem has truth, but only partial truth. There is much more.

FIVE

GETTING TO THE REAL ME

Most people wrestle with poor self-esteem. Many have periodic pangs of insecurity. If man's way of building self-esteem is at best temporary or shallow, is there a better route? Scores of people are finding the answer is *yes*.

Scripture says, "Be ye transformed by the renewing of your mind" (Romans 12:2, KJV). "Transformed" is taken from the Greek word *metamorphoo*.

View the picture—an ugly crawling worm enwraps itself with a cocoon. A beautiful butterfly appears.

Paul is saying, "Be ye metamorphosed." Be ye butterflied. You and I don't have to be enslaved by a poor self-image. Paul is disagreeing here with much of psychology which seeks to help people cope. "Be ye metamorphosed," not "I'll help you cope." Praise the Lord! I don't have to be stuck with this fragile, easily threatened self-image I've carried around all these years. There is hope for drastic change.

"He will perfect that which concerns me" (Psalm 138:8). My self-image concerns me, and God will perfect it.

In that promise lies all the hope in the world for building positive self-esteem, resulting in deep changes within.

INSIGHT—ACTION

Building positive self-esteem is balanced between insight and action. Insight in this sense calls for mind transformation, viewing life from God's perspective, replacing our narrow, negative, self-centered perspective of life. It involves the Holy Spirit at work in our minds and in our hearts as we study God's Word. Life awareness begins to change from "I don't feel very good about myself" to "the Creator of the universe is alive in me."

From this growing insight comes action. Probably the best counseling manual is the book of Ephesians. The first three chapters are basically insight into who we really are, our inheritance in Christ, building self-esteem. We are adopted, accepted, built, capped off with that fantastic promise: "Glory be to God who by his mighty power at work within us is able to do far more than we would ever dare to ask or even dream of—infinitely beyond our highest prayers, and desires, thoughts, or hopes" (Ephesians 3:20).

Action means putting what we see in the first three chapters into shoe leather, as described in the last three chapters of Ephesians. What a great balance to successful living! Three chapters of dynamic *insight* are followed by three chapters of practical application or *action*.

But it's so much easier to walk if there is first an *insight* background. Present-day Christianity is so works-oriented that little ink will be given in this writing to *action* concepts of building positive self-esteem. Emphasis will be on insight, developing God's perspective of our circumstances.

Those of us with poor self-esteem must ask ourselves, "Are we desperate to change?" Does our prayer book read, "God, I don't like myself; I don't feel good about myself. I want to change"?

Personal growth begins when we see a need. If we don't need to see a change in our self-image, then there won't be much growth. But if there is a need, there is hope for growth in positive identity. Matthew recorded Christ's words: "Happy are those who long to be just and good, for they shall be completely satisfied." The writer of Hebrews said: "He [God] rewards those who sincerely look for him."

Many of us feel like praying: "God, you command me to love myself; yet, I don't even like myself. Change my view of myself. Show me who you really created, so that I can remove this distorted picture I have of myself."

One of my clients once told me: "Last night I was studying material on knowing who I am in Christ. I was reading Romans 6, 7, 8, and Charles Solomon's book *Handbook to Happiness* (Wheaton: Tyndale House, 1971) saying, 'Lord, you must meet my need.' At 1 A.M. the Lord spoke to me and showed me who I really was in him. It wasn't an audible voice, but an enlightened awareness. Since then, the sky has never been bluer or the grass greener!"

One man shared a similar experience: "I threw myself prostrate on the ground and said, 'God, you must meet me. You must change this rotten self-image.'" His experience also was climactic. "God showed me who I really was as his child. It was exciting."

Most of us don't have those kinds of experiences. We see a need, study and pray, and move into an "Aha experience." "Ah, yes, I see. I see the person God really created."

Whether it is the climactic experience or the "aha awareness" of who we really are is not the issue. Both springboards involve a process of growth thereafter that takes time. But I do see that the more desperate people are for change, the more quickly changes come.

SLUMS AND SKYSCRAPERS

Building positive self-esteem from God's perspective must be approached like building a skyscraper in a large metropolitan city center where a slum area now stands.

Before the skyscraper can be built the slums have to be cleaned out. Before we begin to build a positive, strong, godly self-esteem, there has to be some urban renewal. Hurts, hates, fears, worries, resentments, guilts that we have been lugging around, conscious and unconscious, must be surfaced and resolved. Consequently, we'll examine a concept called "book of remembrance," cleaning out the slums in our lives.

BOOK OF REMEMBRANCE

So often our backgrounds determine how we feel about ourselves. Being half Estonian, I am fortunate to have an ancestry of slavery. Ewald Palasma, my uncle, has done extensive research in the background of the Estonian people.

He reports that Estonians appeared on the scene about the year 1000. In the year 1219 they were defeated by Denmark. The people and land were sold to the Teutonic Knights, Order of the Sword, who were from the province of Saxony in Germany. In later wars, Russia took over the land and people.

From 1219 to 1819, the Estonians were in virtual slavery and could be sold at any time. In 1819, they were made serfs and could not be sold but had to remain on the land. In 1862, a civil war broke out and they were freed. After 1862, many of the Estonians migrated to other parts of Russia and to America. Schools were started for Estonian education at that time.

Six hundred years of slavery, longer than any other race of people who have been kept in slavery! My mother was the grand-daughter of a slave. What does that make me?

What does that do to my self-esteem? Does that mean that I must live with an aura of slavery that tells me I'm inferior? Or do I take that background of slavery and turn it into something very positive and dynamic?

Everything I have, the Lord and I have achieved. Nothing was handed to me on a silver platter by my forefathers. I can hold my head high. My parents set the example of hard work and integrity. I've followed through. I stand with dignity.

It's sad to see some with a slavery background who have gone the opposite direction by expecting the government to take care of them. They cheer when a president with differing political ideas is shot. Their view of life is a negative "gimme all I want." Self-esteem is zero! Some ethnic leaders in America are deploring how the hand-out system here has really hurt many of their people.

Do I take my background and be controlled by it negatively or do I take the negative parts of my background and use them very positively? It's my choice.

"Hold it, Burwick," someone might say. "Didn't the Apostle Paul tell us not to look back?" The Apostle wrote, "Forgetting the past and looking forward to what lies ahead...." We must forgive and forget the past. It is true. God forgives, so we must also.

Usually the person who regards his background the most negatively is the person who has been hurt so badly that he doesn't want to face it, so he covers up the hurt and avoids it. The reaction is very negative when I suggest the need to go through a book of remembrance.

An intelligent doctor sat in my office, telling me of the trauma he and his wife were going through with their teenage son. I saw that the trouble was really with the father, not the teenager.

I began to probe the physician's relationship with his own father. He had only good things to say about him. But I noticed his wife acting strangely, so I asked her what was wrong. She blurted out the story of a sordid relationship her husband had with his father as a child. At first he denied it, but then he rationalized and made excuses for his father.

I felt I was hitting pay dirt. I knew he was emotionally strong enough to take hard, deep probing. His wife joined me in the psychological surgery. We cut through many layers of defense mechanisms of excusing, intellectualizing, and avoiding. But a massive tumor of painful memories blocked the route to healing. He said, "That's enough," and the session was over. He later told his wife our probing was ridiculous. It was the son who had the problem, he said.

However, as the weeks went on, the pressure kept building. Two months later, he walked into my office: "I guess I need help." I began to probe again. For the first time he broke and began to weep. "Ray, it's too painful. Is there any other way to handle my problems without going back through my memories?" I told him we didn't focus on the past, but before we could focus on solving present problems, he had to make sure contamination from the past was resolved. But he couldn't take it. The physician didn't return.

We need to remind ourselves that self-concept is built through all of our experiences. Experiences, though forgotten, nevertheless still influence the way we think and feel about ourselves. It is not merely a lot of morbid introspection, digging, and trying to find out what is wrong in our past. It is to see if there is some garbage that we are carrying around from our past which is stifling us from building a positive, dynamic, self-esteem.

The purpose of the book of remembrance is to allow the Holy Spirit to bring to the surface the garbage that destroys positive self-esteem, bringing to consciousness the hurt, resentment, and guilt. The purpose for this is so that we can zero in on the circumstances long enough to bear the reality of the hurt or guilt of the situation or person. We shouldn't rationalize or excuse with such explanations as, "Well, she didn't know any better." We must bear the reality of that particular hurt.

Once we have recognized the hurt, we then shift focus from the hurt to our reaction to it. We must accept personal responsibility for our reaction to the wrong, the hurt. We don't continue to blame our ex-husband for what he did. We stop blaming mothers for slapping us when we were two years old when we stuttered or did something else. We won't blame our father for such and such, we won't blame God for our circumstances or for giving us ski-jump noses. We accept personal responsibility for our reactions.

Then begins the forgiving process—resolving the resentments. There are fears, guilts, and insecurities out of childhood, too, but one of the greatest detriments to positive self-esteem is the pack of resentment, bitterness, hurt, and hate that most of us carry.

The forgiveness process is covered in my book *Anger: Defusing the Bomb* (Wheaton: Tyndale House, 1981). David Augsburger's *Freedom of Forgiveness* (Chicago: Moody Press, 1977) is another book I recommend to most of my clients to understand the dynamics of forgiveness.

Here is how we should handle crippling resentments: (1) We pray, "Father, show me any resentment I may be coddling." Much of our resentment is buried in the subconscious. (2) Then, as resentments surface, we pray, "Now, Lord, I need your grace even to want to forgive." Paul Tournier, a dynamic Swiss psychiatrist, believes that it is nearly impossible to forgive. He says that even in Christianity there is very little in-depth forgiveness going on.

As Christians, we can say, "Lord, that hurt was traumatic. In my own strength, I cannot forgive and maybe don't even want to. Give me your power, your life, your grace to be able to forgive, or to want to forgive, that person. You forgive through me."

The Lord's Prayer reads, "Forgive us our sins, just as we have forgiven those who have sinned against us." Thus, the sequence is to forgive those who have wronged us so we can seek God's forgiveness for our sins.

"What my husband did to me was definitely wrong," someone might say. "I'm in the process of forgiving him so, Lord, forgive me for my bitterness for the way he has wronged me."

Some have a hard time forgiving themselves. But there is a solution. We may look in the mirror and say, "Lord, because you have forgiven me and because you are forgiving through me, I choose to forgive the one who offended me. I'll hold it against him no longer." If God forgives me, who am I not to forgive myself!

Then out of the forgiveness dynamic comes healing. The Psalmist wrote, "He heals the broken hearted, binding up their wounds" (Psalm 147:3).

"That hurt was so painful, Lord. Heal that scar," we have every right to pray. Or, we might go to a person whom we trust and say, "Please pray with me for healing of hurts and scars of the past."

If there is a problem between you and someone else, and if that other person knows that you have been carrying bitterness and resentment toward him, you go to him and say, "Will you forgive me for my part of the conflict we have, for the impaired relationship?"

As the memory of a particular hurt resurfaces, it is acknowledged. It is not dwelt upon. "Yes, that hurt, but I'm in the process of forgiving. I choose to remember it no more against him. I'm willing to forget."

The forgiveness process is complete when we can examine the situation and give thanks for it. "All things work together for good. ..." When we are really forgiving, we can see the good that results even from such a hurtful situation.

"Because of what happened, I'm a more forgiving, patient,

understanding person. I'm a stronger person because of it. Thanks," we will be able to say to God.

Forgiveness is then complete. The bucket of bitterness is empty. It must be filled with something else, perhaps active love.

"Lord, love him through me." We look for ways to express that love—the phone call, baked cake, reaching out, being vulnerable even to further hurts or rejection. One client said, "I don't have to fear rejection now that I know I have the resource to forgive."

Total forgiveness means accepting our past, accepting that slavery background, accepting the hurts and traumas of childhood, accepting that alcoholic father who rejected us so cruelly, or accepting that dominating, rigid, controlling mother who made us feel inadequate—accepting our past, and accepting our present circumstances.

Dr. King, a kindly, jubilant man of eighty-four years, was asked one day: "Dr. King, what is the reason for your positive, smiling, sunny disposition?"

He thought for a moment and said, "Each morning when I awaken, I make my own weather."

He was accepting the past, the present, and the future. "Lord, the future looks bleak; look at the economy, look at inflation, look at this rotten marriage."

And God responds, "I want to work all things to your good—past, present, and future. What's important is not your circumstance, but your view of that circumstance."

The spider web is an example. Our three children would look at a web three different ways. One would look at the intricacy of the web and be enthralled by it. One would say, "Ooh! Where is the spider?" and the other would say, "Wow! A trampoline!"

How do we look at circumstances? Can we accept them and say, "Lord, thanks for the rotten marriage, thanks for the stuttering, thanks for the hurts of the past. I accept my responsibility for the past, present, and future. I am not going to blame or excuse. I bear the reality of that hurt. I choose to forgive. I choose to see the good that is coming from it. *In light of the resources of God I refuse to accept my limitations.*"

PERSONAL APPLICATION

If some of us want to work through a book of remembrance, we should set aside a certain time each day and work backwards through five-year segments. If we are forty, for instance, we may say: "Lord, surface anything in my past from the ages of thirty-five to forty that is stifling abundant living—hurts, hates, resentments, and guilts. Bring them to conscious awareness."

As God surfaces such material, we should write it down. We call this a negative autobiography. Begin the forgiveness process with each item that appears. If we can, we should "re-feel" those situations, recall the pain, the hurt, the anger, and the sadness. One of two things will occur. The process will produce deep depression or a sense of release and freedom. The forgiveness process should lift the depression within days. If not, we should see a biblical counselor who can help us work through it.

Within days or a few weeks, there will be a new sense of freedom. Paul wrote, "Forgetting those things which are behind... I press on..." (Philippians 3:14, KJV). We then pray, "Father, if there is any more garbage of my past that needs to surface, you bring it to mind for resolution. I'm living now and am anticipating what you will be doing in and through me."

One client reported this experience: "It is amazing what one week has done to my self-image and peace of mind. I'm a new person. Here's what happened.

"As I began to write the hurts and rejections of my childhood, it was as though I was reliving my past. Oh, did it hurt! I kept writing. I became more and more depressed. There were very painful scenes appearing that I had buried for years.

"I got on my knees and told God I couldn't take it any longer. The pain was too deep, the bitterness too vile, the hurt indescribable. He must step in and do something.

"Dr. Burwick, it wasn't an audible voice, but it seemed as

though God was talking to me: 'My child, you have experienced great hurt and rejection. Let me walk through this with you. I'll give you the grace to deeply forgive and accept these people and circumstances. I brought you through all this for a purpose. I'll use it in your life for something very good.'

"A great peace settled over me. As I faced all I had written, a desire and ability to forgive took over. As I began forgiving those who had really wronged me, it seemed as though shackles began to burst open. I began sensing a freedom I've never known.

"I realize there's more inside. Forgiveness isn't finished. But oh, I feel so much better about myself and life in general."

Many of my clients have profited from the *Forgiveness Process* listing at the end of the chapter.

Step 1 is *awareness*. To some this is no problem. Bitterness runs rampant for all to see. There is total awareness of the need to forgive.

However, many are unaware of resentment, of their need to forgive someone. It is important that a part of the daily quiet time with God be "Search me, God. Make me aware of any grudge, any unforgiving spirit I may carry." This is actually the most important reason for the negative autobiography.

As awareness occurs, we should write the names of those needing to be forgiven on the process sheet according to where they fit at the moment.

"Dad really blew it as a father. He spent no time with me. He called me names, abused my mother. There's no way I'll forgive him," someone might say. Consequently, Dad's name is placed by Step 2, *need for desire* to forgive.

"God, I don't want to forgive him. Soften my heart. Give me a desire even to want to forgive Dad." This is prayed daily. God not only helps us obey but helps us want to obey (Philippians 2:13).

At times God softens our heart by reminding us how much he has to forgive us; so, who are we not to forgive another?

At other times he gently suggests that our lack of peace can be resolved by forgiving.

The desire to forgive does come, and the person's name is moved down to Step 3.

I suggest that you not hurry to Step 3. There is very little deep forgiving taking place in the lives of most Christians.

There are many "shoulds" and "oughts." "I forgive" is glibly mouthed, because we know we should. There must be a brutal honesty to admit, "That really did hurt. It's going to cost me a dear price to set you free from that rejection debt. You wronged me terribly. I choose to begin to remember it against you no longer. I choose to wipe your slate clean."

Our feelings say, "Don't." However, by an act of our will we ask God to work through us what we can't do ourselves. "Father, forgive through me," we should pray daily until there is a sense of freedom toward the person.

The decision has been made to forgive. We can then incorporate Step 4, *confession*. "God, forgive me for my reaction of resentment." God doesn't forgive us if we are not forgiving others (Matthew 6:15).

Step 5 involves asking forgiveness of another if that person knows of our bad attitude toward him. "Yes, I've forgiven the elder in our church with whom I had a blowout. But I haven't asked him to forgive me." His name is written by Step 5.

In the dynamics of forgiveness, there may be the need to forgive oneself, Step 6. "If God forgives me of my sin, who am I not to forgive me?"

"Dr. Burwick, does it mean I haven't forgiven if I still remember the hurtful incident?" is a question I often hear. I answer, "Though you have begun the forgiveness process, maybe the process isn't finished or, maybe you have forgiven and the memory which remains is just the *fact* of the issue without any contamination of resentful, hurt feelings." Our amazing brains, which can absorb hundreds of memories per second, never really forget anything.

When a memory surfaces it is wise to say, "Yes, that did hurt. I'm not denying that. However, I'm in the process of forgiving. Consequently, I'm *willing to forget*." "Forget" here would mean refusing to keep score, retaining no judgmental attitude.

How do we know when we have really forgiven someone? It seems as though the following barometer is an accurate indicator.

Forgiveness is complete when I can silently say, "Thanks for what you did to me." For example, I'm now able to say, "Mom, you wronged me in regard to stuttering. I resented you for it. But as my forgiveness process is completed, I can thank you for your mistakes. They've driven me deeply into God. Because of stuttering, I'm a good listener. I depend on God for the ability to speak. I understand pain, and that helps me as a counselor. I'm a more forgiving person, and I could go on. Thanks, Mom." Forgiveness is then complete.

Resentment is cleansed by forgiveness, but must be replaced by *love in action*, Step 9, giving, caring, sharing, not expecting anything in return. We ought to pray over this list daily and follow our prayer with attitudes and actions that indicate forgiveness and love in action.

As our resentment becomes cleared out, we can receive what God has to say about us and positive self-esteem grows.

Forgiveness Process

1. AWARENESS
2. NEED FOR DESIRE
3. DECISION
4. CONFESSION
5. RESTITUTION
6. FORGIVE SELF
7. WILLING TO FORGET
8. THANKS—PRAISE
9. LOVE IN ACTION

SIX

MY HERITAGE

A young man once asked his father, "How do I stack up worthwise?"

The greatest weakness in American Christians is that we don't know God our Father. Consequently, we don't know our worth because of this relationship. We spend much time in a lot of religious activities, but we don't know God.

A. W. Tozer declared that "the understanding of God is so decadent as to be utterly beneath the dignity of the Most High God." The words "Be still and know that I am God" had become meaningless to the bustling, self-confident Christians he knew. They were more interested in living a victorious life than in knowing God.

P. T. Forsyth observed that "the nontheological Christ is popular. He wins votes, but he is not mighty. He does not win souls. He does not break men into small pieces and create them anew."

Who is God? What does God have to do with my self-esteem?

An English magazine advertisement pictured a dog and a cat lying side by side in harmony. The legend over the picture stated: "A couple of 'VIPs,' very important pets. What makes them important is who owns them."

What makes you and me important is who owns us. The Psalmist wrote, "It is [God] that hath made us, and not we ourselves; we are his people . . ." (Psalm 100:3, KJV).

The New Testament states it this way:

"And because we are his sons God has sent the Spirit of his Son into our hearts, so now we can rightly speak of God as our dear Father. Now we are no longer slaves, but God's own sons. And since we are his sons, everything he has belongs to us, for that is the way God planned."

Think of it! Everything God has is ours. As one man said, "We pull our chair up to God's table and say, 'Pass the biscuits.' " All his resources are at my disposal!

As we look at this mind-blowing concept every day, think of the dynamic influence on our self-esteem! All his resources are ours!

A young businessman sat in my office, head in hands, weeping. He sobbed, "Why can't my dad love me?" Though successful, and appearing very calm, confident, and witty, Peter had a raging inner battle. His life was chaotic—he was filled with anxiety, depression, obsessive fears, and stuttering.

Here's what I found out:

His mother was deceitful, had shown him no affection or attention. She even made the statement to Peter: "I didn't have to have you" (implying abortion). She was very critical of Peter and his dad, and hateful.

His father was extremely critical. "I can't even wear the right clothes to please him," Peter said. He showed no expression of love or encouragement. When confronted with this previously by Peter, his dad's response was, "You're going to get the million-dollar business. What more do you want?"

Peter's reply was, "I'd sweep Highway 78 with a whiskbroom if you'd tell me you love me."

Peter described himself as "rotten, a nobody" and felt totally rejected.

Therapy obviously had to change self-perspective. We began by surfacing the hate with which he was consumed.

"When people don't react the way I want them to, I hate them," he said.

Weeks were spent just beginning the forgiveness process. It didn't come easy for Peter. Fear shackled him. His thinking was irrational and distorted. He would often ask how he could let go of hate.

Progress came as Peter viewed in his mind a personal banquet table. God sat at the head of the bountifully laden spread. "Now, Peter, God is your loving Father. He wants to give you more than you can even dream of. Ask him to pass the biscuits."

As Peter studied appropriate Scripture and visualized this every day, his outlook on life became much more positive. He said, "When I hit a snag during the day, like having a crazy fear, I quickly visualize the banquet table and ask my Father to pass the biscuits. Fear subsides."

At times hate would erupt and pour out its molten lava. "I'd lie on my bed and want to scream, curse, kick, and punch. At times I'd carry it out. I would want to let go of the hate and resolve it by forgiving, yet a part of me just wouldn't let go.

"God would bring more old hurtful memories to my mind. More hate would gush out. Finally in total exhaustion and desperation I'd visualize myself at the banquet table: 'Here, Father, I give you these people who have really wronged me. I give you the hate. Take it, and pass the biscuit of forgiving others.'

"Oh, the freedom and peace that comes! And it lasts, till I let irritations build up. Those lead to volcanic eruptions and I have to repeat the process."

At the beginning of our seventh session, Peter told me excitedly, "My visualization is changing. I'm no longer a little boy at the banquet table. Now I'm a grown son. I'm actually feeling grown up for the first time. I'm beginning to like me."

Knowing the Father, the God to whom Peter was being introduced, is both personal and majestic. Nowhere in the Bible more than in the first chapters of Genesis do we see the personal nature of God expressed. God deliberated with himself when he said "Let us" in Genesis 1:26. He brought the animals to Adam to see what Adam would call them. He walked in the garden calling to Adam; he talked; he asked people questions; he came down from heaven in order to find out what men were doing. He was so grieved by human wickedness that he repented of making men.

Presentations of God like these are meant to bring home to us the fact that the God with whom we have to do is not just a mere cosmic principle, impersonal and indifferent, but a living person —thinking, feeling, active, approving of good, disapproving of evil, and interested in his creatures all the time.

Do you want more and more of God's kindness and peace? Then learn to know him better and better. For as you know him better, he will give you, through his great power, everything you need for living a truly good life: he even shares his own glory and his own goodness with us! And by that same mighty power he has given us all the other rich and wonderful blessings he promised; for instance, the promise to save us from the lust and rottenness all around us, and to give us his own character (2 Peter 1:2-4).

He gives us his own character. What self-image! But what is the prerequisite? Knowing God better and better. As we know God better, he gives us his own character.

In the Old Testament, Hosea wrote: "Oh, that we might know the Lord! Let us press on to know him. And he will respond to us as surely as the coming of dawn, or the rain of early spring. . . . I don't want your sacrifices—I want your love; I don't want your offerings—I want you to know me" (Hosea 6:3, 6).

God, my Father, my Owner, is saying, "I want you to know me so that I can bless you."

But Christianity is so often a mass of activity—going and doing—deeply involved but not providing the time to "be still and know that I am God."

I often talk with "burned-out" Christians. I am thinking of a young doctor who many years ago was active in church. He was there every time the doors opened. He was witnessing. He was at all the Bible studies. But all of a sudden, he quit. He got tired. He burned out. Because his emphasis was on doing, he forgot to know God, to know his resources in Christ.

Self-oriented activity often ends in catastrophe. We need to remind ourselves of the balance. The Apostle Paul wrote:

[I ask] that the way you live will always please the Lord and honor him, so that you will always be doing good, kind things for others, while all the time you are learning to *know* God better and better (Colossians 1:10).

The balance is *doing* and *knowing God*. Jeremiah wrote:

Let them boast in this alone: that they truly know me, and understand that I am the Lord of justice and righteousness whose love is steadfast; and that I love to be this way (Jeremiah 9:24).

J. I. Packer states it this way in his book *Knowing God:*

> We are cruel to ourselves if we try to live in this world without knowing about the God whose world it is and who runs it. The world becomes a strange and painful place and life in it is a disappointing and unpleasant business for those who do not know about God. Disregard the study of God and you sentence yourself to stumble and blunder through life blindfolded, as it were, with no sense of direction and no understanding of what surrounds you. This way you can waste your life and lose your soul.

Who is God? The Westminster Shorter Catechism states: "God is a Spirit, infinite, eternal and unchangeable in his being, wisdom, power, holiness, justice, goodness, and truth." Isaiah wrote:

> I am Jehovah; there is no other God. I will strengthen you and send you out to victory even though you don't know me, and all the world from east to west will know there is no other God. I am Jehovah and there is no one else. I alone am God. I form the light and make the dark. I send the good times and bad. I, Jehovah, am he who does these things (Isaiah 45:5-7).

God is the same yesterday, today, and forever.

> [The Lord asks] Was I too weak to save you? Is that why the house is silent and empty when I come home? Have I no longer power to deliver? No, that is not the reason! For I can rebuke the sea and make it dry! I can turn the rivers into deserts, covered with dying fish. I am the one who sends the darkness out across the skies (Isaiah 50:2, 3).

My Father! Your Father! What does that do to self-esteem? Like the little boy who pulled himself up and said, "That is *my* daddy," insinuating that because he is "my daddy" that makes him significant.

Because of my Father I am significant.

God desires that we know him. *Vines Expository Dictionary* lists a number of Greek roots for the word "know," but there is a general definition that states: "to take knowledge, to recognize, to understand." It indicates a relationship between the person knowing and the object known. It is a relationship where two people know each other well.

In Spokane, Washington, I held a premarital workshop with ten engaged couples. Each couple took a personality test that helped them begin really to know each other. By the time the workshop was over, five of the couples decided not to get married. I thought it was a successful experience.

They decided not to get married because their relationship had been built on a very shallow foundation with a lot of physical involvement. There was little communication on a soul level, such as sharing hurts, angers, fears, goals. They spent little time together in prayer and Bible study. As they began really to know each other, half of them decided they didn't want to commit their lives to each other.

A relationship involves knowing, the kind of knowledge that comes not by mere thinking, but by operation of the Holy Spirit subsequent to acceptance of Christ. We lay hold of the truth of really knowing God after we take that first step of salvation: "Lord Jesus, come into my life. Forgive my sins. Make me a new person." To those who have made the discovery of knowing Christ personally, who have received him, he gives the right to become children of God (John 1:12). Those who have made this discovery and have involved themselves with Christ should be in the process of making the discovery of knowing God.

Four concepts in knowing God are the base on which to build positive self-esteem. The first is to *study Scripture*, not so much from the perspective of knowing doctrines and stories of the Bible as for meeting the Author. Doctrine is important, but knowing the Author is of utmost importance.

The story of the fiery furnace in the book of Daniel is exciting. It shows what God can do. As we become more mature in our Christian walk, we read the same story and gain a different perspective. The only thing that was burnt were their fetters. God takes us into fiery furnaces to burn off our fetters of insecurity, lust, pride, and anger. Look what God does for his children. And he is our Father! If he did that for Shadrach, Meshach, and Abednego, he wants to use our fiery furnaces right now, our marriage turmoils, our business problems, our child-rearing challenges, to burn off some of our fetters. Because he is our loving heavenly Father, he is keeping us in the furnace just long enough to burn the fetters of self that bind us from receiving his blessing. First Corinthians 10:13 reminds us that God won't let the fire get too hot.

I am counseling a bright young physician who has personal and family problems. He is in a legalistic church where doctrines of do's and don'ts are emphasized. He reported, "I have studied Scripture knowing all the doctrines, but for the first time I am getting to meet the Author." I could see relaxation replacing the tenseness in his facial muscles. To know the Author and realize the resources we have in him is our challenge in building positive self-esteem.

We should study Scripture from the perspective of knowing the Author. For instance, the first six chapters of the book of Daniel repeat over and over "The Lord gave," or "God gave." The *Lord gave* victory over Jehoiakim. *God had given* the superintendent a special appreciation for Daniel. *God gave* these four youths great ability to learn and they soon mastered all the literature and science of the times. *God gave* to Daniel special ability to understand the meanings of dreams and visions. *God told* Daniel what the king had dreamed.

World events are in God's control. He removes kings and sets others on their thrones. He gives wise men their wisdom and scholars their intelligence. He reveals profound mysteries beyond man's understanding. This is our Father. God is the same—yesterday, today, and forever.

The second basic concept in knowing God is to "taste and see," a personal involvement with God. The Psalmist wrote: "Taste and see that the Lord is good" (Psalm 34:8). We should study Scripture with anticipation to know his ways of thinking and feeling, his reactions, his disposition, in order to develop a close fellowship.

As Paul wrote, " . . . that I may know him, and the power of his resurrection, and the fellowship of his sufferings" (Philippians 3:10, KJV). To know God better we might memorize such verses as: "Fear not, for I am with you. Do not be dismayed. I am your God. I will strengthen you; I will help you; I will uphold you with my victorious right hand" (Isaiah 41:10).

We can use this truth. All hell is breaking loose economically. Some of us are facing possible bankruptcy when not many months ago we were flourishing. Does Isaiah 41:10 apply?

Some of us are going through some real trauma in our families. It is so easy to focus on the circumstances and forget: "I am your God. I will strengthen you. I will uphold you with my victorious right hand" (no matter how the circumstances appear).

Some of us are wrestling with poor self-esteem. A few years ago I was speaking at an Oral Roberts University chapel service. The Lord was close and I felt almost lifted up as I spoke. It was very exciting. Then they invited me to the cafeteria for the noon luncheon.

It was a large room. I walked through the food line and then faced a mass of people, tables, and chairs. I was extremely bothered by a fragile self-esteem at the time. So as I took my food tray and began to enter that mass of people, I was shaking. "I wonder if my tie is straight. What do they think of me?" It was a typical Don Knotts fear reaction. Suddenly I remembered who I was. "Lord, you are in me. I don't have to be controlled by these poor self-image feelings. You are alive in me. Love these people through me."

As the focus shifted from self to others and God, and as I reminded myself of who I was in Christ, I had peace. The situation was the same but my thinking was different. That was an example of "tasting and seeing that God is good" and using it in practical application.

The next concept in knowing our Father is to count on God's initiative, God's grace. He called us; he saved us; he is in the process of sanctifying us. "I am the good shepherd and know my own sheep, and they know me . . . and I lay down my life for my sheep. . . . My sheep recognize my voice, and I know them. . . . and they shall never perish" (John 10:14, 15, 27, 28).

The implication here is that God is a loving, caring, redeeming, faithful, personal God who watches over his children.

Those of us who are fathers love to do things for our children. We encourage them to develop their musical abilities, their athletic abilities, their academic abilities. We do what we can for them. We go without a new suit of clothes so that they can have a new Easter dress. How much more does our heavenly Father want to do for you and me? So often we don't realize this because we don't know him.

God's initiative reaches out. Yet we must cooperate. My responsibility to know him must be my controlling desire as a Christian. God cannot be known by just two or three minutes of quiet time in the morning or at bedtime. We must be unhurriedly alone with him long enough and often enough for him to fulfill his promises to us: "He that loveth me shall be loved by my Father, and I will love him, and will manifest myself to him" (John 14:21, KJV). To know him must be our dearest and deepest ambition. Think of how easy it is to be controlled by passion for money or lust.

A friend wrestled with severe lust temptations a few years ago. One concept that made lust repulsive to him, which added to his motivation to gain victory over it, was his determination: "If I could be so controlled by the passion for knowing God as I am being tempted and submitting sometimes to that temptation of lust, what kind of a Christian would I be!"

At times lust can be overwhelming and controlling. We embrace it, knowing it is sin. There is temporary pleasure in it. But if we could be controlled by that intense a passion to know God better, what would that do to build positive self-esteem?

Mining for gold must be very exciting. I can imagine sifting rocks and sand through the shaker pan and excitedly awaiting the appearance of gold treasure.

Paul wrote: "In him [Christ] lie hidden all the mighty, untapped treasures of wisdom and knowledge." The treasures are not only in him; notice that they are *hidden* in him.

Are they hidden because God is reluctant to let us taste and see of his treasure of wisdom and knowledge? No. It is that we might have a continual joy of discovery.

How many times have we read Ephesians 1 and observed something new? Notice the profound truths: "Chosen by God; having the inheritance of Christ; adopted into God's family; the same power that raised Christ from the dead is alive in you and me. . . ."

As we mine these treasures of knowing God, we know ourselves better. We see the significance of who we really are. It is not that we are better than anyone else, but because God is our Father, we are his children, and that makes us very significant.

Often in my counseling it is very apparent in one of my clients that a victorious life became stagnant and problems set in when the time they spent daily knowing God became minimal. Because there wasn't that meaningful thirty to sixty minutes in dialogue with God, in Bible meditation and prayer, the client forgot who he was and the resources he had.

I counseled a person recently who had a strong urge to drive his car off a cliff. When that urge overwhelmed him, he thought he had better get counseling. I asked him how long cliff-rolling had been a sport for him. He said, "You know, I became a Christian two years ago. The first year was tremendous. I was free from all emotional conflicts. But this last year I've gotten slack in my quiet time with God. Old emotional troubles have begun to resurface."

As we talked, I saw he had forgotten where his resources were. His personal time with God became a hit or miss arrangement. Hurts, resentments, and insecurities grew. Mental trauma surfaced and he found himself at the bottom of a ravine.

How do we know our Father? We walk boldly into the presence

of God and say, "Lord, teach me who you are." The Psalmist wrote: "I will meditate about your glory, splendor, majesty and miracles."

Meditation is the activity of calling to mind, contemplating, thinking over, dwelling on, and applying to oneself, the various concepts that one knows about the promises, purposes, and ways of God. Is this our natural way of thinking?

Imagine having a flat tire on the freeway when it is raining cats and dogs. Is our natural inclination at such a time to dwell on the promises, purposes, and ways of God?

Someone is golfing and shooting a great score going into the last hole. The last tee shot slices way out into the rough. Is the natural tendency at that point to meditate upon the promises, purposes, and ways of God?

We are expecting a raise and the boss says, "Sorry, the budget is too tight."

Someone has never been married and wants very much to find a mate.

A former spouse has promised a certain amount of money but it is not coming through. Is the natural tendency to think upon the promises, purposes, and ways of God?

Look at each of these experiences. Could it be that God has allowed them for a purpose? Consider the flat tire. The person who is going to stop and help may need to hear the message of Jesus Christ.

I remember the last time I played golf, I found that I had to make a decision, to give up either golf or religion, because I lost my religion every time I played golf. In my angry fits I threw the club farther than I had hit the ball. That was not the way a Christian should act.

I was on the tee with one ball left. An ugly rough loomed on the right, protected by a barbed wire fence. You guessed it. Right smack in the middle of high weeds and bushes, behind the fence, landed my little white ball.

A miracle happened. I said, "Well, Lord, that was my last ball. Chances are slim that I'll find it. But, thanks."

My golfing partner almost dropped his clubs. "What did you say?"

I repeated myself and told him that I had been learning to give thanks in all things. Then I climbed through the fence hoping to find my wayward ball and found six new golf balls. "Thank you, Lord."

Reminding ourselves of the promises, purposes, and ways of God shows us how significant we are, and it removes much stress from us.

We put ourselves under much pressure by looking at life from our self-centered, negative viewpoint instead of looking at life from the view of our Father, realizing that all things work together for good. He is conforming us to the image of his Son through flat tires, golf shots, divorce—everything.

We must eliminate thoughts that limit God, that make him small. As we meditate on Scriptures such as Psalm 139, we can see the majesty and dynamics of our Father.

Christ said that if we know him, we will know the Father. Consequently, the second way to know him is to study the Gospels so that we become acquainted with the character of Christ. By knowing his character, we will know the character of God our Father. Jesus was *tough*, driving the religious materialists out of the temple. He was *tender*, weeping over Lazarus. He was *wise*, diagnosing the heart of man. He was *compassionate*, caring for the adulterous woman. He was *righteous*, condemning the Pharisees.

The fourth way to know God is to compare him with the great powers. Do we realize that there are four billion plus inhabitants on earth? Earth is a minute part of its galaxy, and there are thousands of galaxies. All of creation is God's footstool. There are millions of stars, billions of light years apart—God's footstool. Yet he is interested in us. He is our Father, whose eye is never off of us. There is no moment when his care for us falters, no matter how passively or actively we resist him.

God our Father wants a personal relationship with us. This

begins with making the discovery of knowing his Son, Christ, asking him to dwell within us—forgiving our sins, making us a new person, turning us from ourselves to him. We must get to know him by spending time with him. As we know him we know the supernatural resources available to us. We learn who we really are. This is the basis for our attitudes and actions, the basis for building positive self-esteem.

PERSONAL APPLICATION

To get a deeper awareness of who God our Father really is, here are some suggestions:

First, we should write a short description of how we picture our earthly father with the eyes of a child. Was he gone all the time? Our writing might describe him as absent or almost nonexistent. Was he cruel, hot-tempered, or did he verbally assassinate us? No father is perfect. We shouldn't excuse him for any of his weaknesses, as it will hinder this project and stifle our wholeness.

Next, we should write our view of God. How do we picture him? After we have done this, we should compare the two fathers. Most people find there is a close relationship or correlation between how they see their earthly father and heavenly Father. Because no father is perfect, there is usually a flaw in how we view God. This view of God must be changed in our quest for building positive self-esteem.

Changing our view of God involves two corrective measures. First, we make sure we have completed the forgiveness process toward our earthly father, freeing us from any negative bonds with him.

Second, we must reprogram our mental computer. We should study Scripture with the goal in mind of knowing God. The book of Isaiah and Joshua 1—11 are excellent places to start, along with 2 Chronicles 20.

As my own children worked through this project, they made comments such as, "My heavenly Father is not harsh, perfectionistic, stingy, demanding, critical. My heavenly Father is. . . ."

We should set aside thirty to sixty minutes daily to talk to our heavenly Father and let him talk to us through his Word, the Bible.

An excellent book to read to know more about God and his work in our lives is J. I. Packer's *Knowing God* (Downers Grove, IL: InterVarsity, 1972).

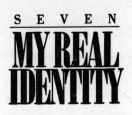

SEVEN

MY REAL IDENTITY

In the last chapter we saw that building positive self-esteem is based upon knowing God our Father. God, whose footstool is four billion inhabitants of earth, thousands of galaxies, millions of stars that are billions of light years in distance, is interested in us. Isn't that fantastic?

Our Father, whose eye is never off us, allows no moment for his care to falter. He works all things to our good. He seeks to give us his own character. Think what this can do toward building positive self-esteem as our minds are saturated with these concepts.

Self-consciousness does not give us our true identity, because we might think we are Cleopatra or Alexander the Great. In my counseling I meet people who think they are the Virgin Mary or Jesus the Messiah. Self-consciousness doesn't tell us who we are.

Achievement, looking well, and thinking positively are only partial answers to true identity. Basing our self-esteem on how we think other people think of us can have a devastating yo-yo effect. "I feel significant when Bob strokes me. I feel inadequate if Wayne criticizes me or ignores me" are examples of the yo-yo experience.

True identity is what we are from God's perspective. That which we are to examine now is the most dynamic, life-changing concept I have ever seen. It has done more for my personal growth and family development than any other concept to which I've been exposed. As my clients begin to understand it and put it into practice I see more changes in people's lives from this one concept than anything else.

In Colossians we read that Paul was sent to help the church and to tell God's secret plan. "He has kept this secret for centuries and generations past, but now at last it has pleased him to tell it to those who love him and live for him, and the riches and glory of his plan are for you Gentiles too. And this is the secret: that Christ in your hearts is your only hope of glory" (Colossians 1:26-28).

Paul was saying, "I have a secret for you. It is a mystery, and I want to tell you what it is." As I observe Christianity now, I think that it is still a well kept secret.

Christ is in you. Our hope of glory—what does that mean? It seems as though much of Christianity is based on performing, doing, trying to build up self, to live for Christ. There is so much frustration, emptiness, and defeat among Christians. The secret —what is the secret?

Need precedes understanding this mystery. Need may come from some personal trauma, a marriage upheaval, a child-rearing challenge, emotional and mental problems, business reversals, or from an awareness that the abundant Christian life is impossible for us to live.

Matthew described the supernatural life-style: turn the other cheek. If someone wants your coat, give him your shirt. Love your enemies. Even the most distorted personality doesn't naturally want to love an enemy. Our natural inclination, even though we may be strong, mature Christians, is to get even or withdraw.

"I can't live the Christian life as Christ commanded" or "This pain is too severe" provides a sense of need. "I need something more. I can't go on like this."

Let us examine who we really are and see if there is a way to meet our need. Is there a way to live supernaturally? Three aspects of our personhood are: who we were before Christ; what happened when we became Christians; and who we are now.

THE DIVINE EXCHANGE

The tri-circle has been used by many authors to diagram the material and immaterial parts of man. Though there is disagreement as to whether man is of two parts (dichotomy) or three parts (trichotomy), I prefer to think of man as being of three parts. Man is depicted at least one time in Scripture as being of three parts: "And the very God of peace sanctify you wholly; and I pray God your whole spirit and soul and body be preserved blameless unto the coming of our Lord Jesus Christ" (1 Thessalonians 5:23, KJV). In speaking of the makeup of a non-Christian, the Scriptures refer to his spirit as the "old man" or the "old nature." Positionally he is spoken of as being "in Adam."

Spirit. Man's spirit is dead to God (separated from God); his soul and body are alive to self and controlled by Satan. Paul described the condition: "And you hath he quickened [made alive] who were dead in trespasses and sins; wherein time past ye walked according to . . . the prince of the power of the air [Satan], the spirit that now worketh in the children of disobedience: Among whom also we had our conversation [manner of life] in times past in the lusts of our flesh, fulfilling the desires of the flesh and of the mind; and were by nature the children of wrath, even as others" (Ephesians 2:1-3, KJV).

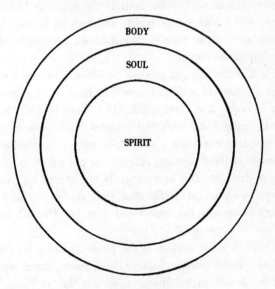

In the "old man,"
the spirit, separated from God,
is described as being dead.

Body. On the surface, before Christ, the body is seen as that which executes the business of the soul. Besides its physiological functions, the body is the home of the five senses and basic drives. It is a "space suit" containing the real person. A man is not a body; he lives in one.

Soul. The soul includes the mind, emotions, and the will, the ability to decide. In short, the mind works through the mechanism of the nervous system. As an event occurs, the mind reacts, through the mechanism of the cells of the nervous tissue, and a broad range of things happen, including voluntary and involuntary body movements, along with conscious and unconscious thinking. Another description of the mind is "the consciousness that originates in the brain and directs mental and physical behavior."

The emotional part of the soul is the capacity to experience feelings, which can cause bodily changes in breathing, pulse, glandular secretions, mental disturbances, and many other less discernible phenomena.

The will is the thought process by which a person deliberately chooses a course of action. The will influences all of man.

Man is body, soul, and spirit. He is born in sin. "We started out bad, being born with evil natures, and were under God's anger just like everyone else" (Ephesians 2:3). Paul explained that the sin of the first man, Adam, was passed on to all of us.

Man in this state sins automatically because of his true nature. "Once you were under God's curse, doomed forever for your sins. You went along with the crowd and were just like all the others, full of sin" (Ephesians 2:1, 2).

The world's value system is the guide to living for the person "in Adam." Materialism, pleasure, lust, greed, status seeking are among the self-absorbed characteristics of the "old man."

Paul took it a step further. The nonbeliever not only lives according to the world value system, but is actually obeying Satan. "Ye walked . . . according to the prince of the power of the air [Satan]" (Ephesians 2:2, KJV).

Results of the old nature include

Fear	Pride	Workaholism
Phobias	Criticism	Hatred
Tension	Laziness	Jealousy
Controlling	Defeat	Insecurity
Hypersensitivity	Anger	Self-centeredness
Inhibitions	Guilt	Impatience
Self-effort	Stubbornness	Perfectionism
Worry	Depression	Irresponsibility
Bitterness	Religious fervor	

The ultimate result is hell. "For the wages of sin is death; but the gift of God is eternal life through Jesus Christ, our Lord" (Romans 6:23, KJV).

Because the "old man" is in Adam, he is unresponsive to God's leadership and power, controlled and empowered by self and Satan. Any self-esteem building for the non-Christian must come from self-effort only.

Because the non-Christian has no interest in pleasing and focusing upon God, his mind feeds upon the world, the flesh, and the devil. Pleasure, status, materialism, comfort, self-seeking and self-absorption are natural by-products.

A child, with an Adamic nature, raised by imperfect parents in an imperfect environment, molded by the world value system, controlled by Satan, develops feelings of inferiority, insecurity, and other self-destructive characteristics. Physical disease is also a common result.

Obviously, the better parents a child has, the less he will experience self-esteem distortion. Care, warmth, tenderness, personal involvement, open communication, tough discipline—all help to mold a child with positive self-regard.

Any measure of harshness, leniency, comparing, perfectionism, overprotectiveness, criticalness, rigidness, dominating, conditional love, absence, and humiliating treatment leads to damaged self-esteem.

Another diagrammatical view shows man without Christ. Observe what can happen (see next page).

This diagram shows messages coming through a "body gate," the eye. A woman observes her husband being a little too friendly with the neighbor lady. This triggers thoughts in the *mind* such as: "Hey, what's going on here? He hasn't been very affectionate lately. Could he be getting his affection from her?"

And emotions, such as fear, anger, jealousy spring up. Negative feelings and thoughts continue to grow into explosive, volcanic dimensions.

Notice the arrows leading from *emotions* to *body*. This describes the two avenues our negative emotions can take. Arrows going through and out the body indicate ventilation of feelings through talking, shouting, writing, hitting, or physical exercise. Feelings are released. There is less danger of psychosomatic disease because there are no bottled-up emotions. Venting all the emotions, however, can destroy relationships and hurt others.

Arrows on the right side indicate negative feelings tucked within. Controlling or denying negative emotions is the leading cause of physical, mental, emotional, and spiritual disease.

It begins in the "eye gate," triggering negative thoughts and feelings. It ends up either ventilated or tucked within where it produces ulcers, depression, headaches, and various other ailments.

The spirit dimension in this diagram is labeled "unregenerate." The natural man—the man without Christ—has no other resource upon which to draw. He is limited to his own efforts to solve his problems and challenges. God's Spirit cannot work in his life for he is controlled by Satan, the god of this world.

THE TRANSITION

But man doesn't have to endure this fate. Paul wrote, "But God is so rich in mercy; he loved us so much that even though we were

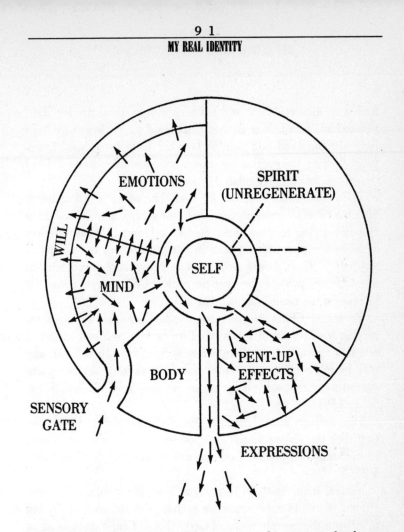

spiritually dead and doomed by our sins, he gave us back our lives again when he raised Christ from the dead" (Ephesians 2:4, 5). To the Colossians he wrote: "For he has rescued us out of the darkness and gloom of Satan's kingdom and brought us into the kingdom of his dear Son, who bought our freedom with his blood and forgave us our sins" (Colossians 1:13, 14).

There can be divine exchange. There is a rescue, a freedom from the shackles of the natural man without Christ. How does this happen?

Jesus said, "No man can come to me, except the Father which

hath sent me draw him: and I will raise him up at the last day" (John 6:44, KJV). It is further elaborated on by Jeremiah: "For long ago the Lord had said to Israel: I have loved you, O my people, with an everlasting love; with lovingkindness I have drawn you to me" (Jeremiah 31:3).

The natural man is drawn by God. Through a sense of need, either a "wreck" or awareness that "something is missing," man responds to the bidding of the Hound of Heaven. "God whispers to us in our pleasures, speaks in our conscience, but shouts in our pains," C. S. Lewis said. "But as many as received him, to them gave he power to become the sons of God, even to them that believe on his name" (John 1:12, KJV).

Receiving Christ involves turning to God from self and receiving his free gift of salvation. Turning from self and sin leads to a new birth. In fact, there is a new creation. "Therefore if any man be in Christ, he is a new creature [creation]; old things are passed away; behold, all things are become new" (2 Corinthians 5:17, KJV).

This new creation is further described four verses later: "For God took the sinless Christ and poured into him our sins. Then, in exchange, he poured God's goodness into us!" (2 Corinthians 5:21).

Natural man, destined to reap, at best, the results of his own efforts, is free to experience the exchange of sin and self, being filled with the completeness of God. "For in Christ there is all of God in a human body; so you have everything when you have Christ, and you are filled with God through your union with Christ. He is the highest Ruler, with authority over every other power" (Colossians 2:9, 10).

THE NEW CREATION

What is this new creation? How does he function? What does he look like? Remember our first diagram depicting natural man without Christ? There is a slight, yet radical, difference in the *New Creation* diagram.

The new creation's body and soul have the same functions and appear the same as before receiving Christ. There are still miles of blood vessels and twenty-four feet of intestines. There is still the tendency to insecurity, impatience, resentment or self-effort. But there is a new master, a new "coach."

The natural man controlled by self and Satan has been replaced by the new creation. At the controls is the Creator of the Universe. The new birth sees a resurrected spirit dimension that exercises control of and renews the mind, which in turn affects emotions, behavior, and bodily functions.

The spirit, indwelt by the Holy Spirit, is coach, the soul is captain, and the body is player. The captain tells the player to carry out functions of the coach. Previously, the body had to function according to self and Satan. Now, the inner man (captain) directed by the indwelling Christ (the Holy Spirit), empowers the body (player) to function at peace with itself and its environment. The coach, with all his experience, wisdom, and power, is actually living through the captain and player, producing supernatural living.

Using the same tri-circle diagram, arrows from the spirit dimension are directed outward to and through soul and body. Love, joy, peace, patience, goodness, kindness, gentleness, self-

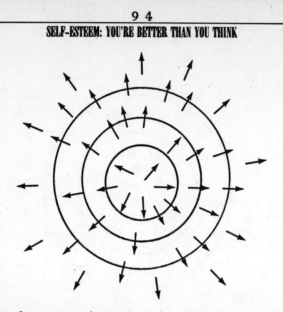

control, adequacy reach out from the coach, not only affecting captain and player's attitudes and behavior, but spreading out to others for a redemptive ministry.

Jealousy, inadequacy, tension, laziness, etc., begin to disappear. Others observe the changing process. Interest is aroused. Others are brought to experience the new birth; spiritual growth is stimulated in dormant Christians because of the change observed in a person growing in Christ.

"Burwick," you may say, "if that's my new creation, why do I still act like the old nature? I still feel insecure, at times explosive, and I also worry." The answer comes as we begin to experience in reality what the Bible says happened when we were born again.

DEATH TO LIFE

Paul wrote, "Knowing this, that our old man is crucified with him, that the body of sin might be destroyed" (Romans 6:6, KJV). To the Galatians Paul wrote, "I am crucified with Christ..." (Galatians 2:20, KJV).

"Crucified" in this context comes from the Greek word *sustauroo*, which means crucifixion in company with another, as the thieves were crucified with Christ. Metaphorically, it refers to spiritual identification with Christ in his death.

Consequently, the person who is born again actually died with Christ. The old, unregenerate spirit is finished. There is now a new creation, a regenerate spirit. "Therefore, if any man be in Christ, he is a new creature: old things are passed away; behold, all things are become new" (2 Corinthians 5:17, KJV).

The person before Christ—the old man, the old nature—is dead. Paul substantiated this: "Now then it is no more I that do it, but sin that dwelleth in me. . . . Now if I do that I would not, it is no more I that do it, but sin that dwelleth in me" (Romans 7:17, 20, KJV).

I believe Paul is saying, "My new creation doesn't sin. But this new creation is embodied in the flesh, in which dwells no good thing."

If I don't say "no" to the flesh, I'll be acting and thinking just as I did before I became a Christian. The result is sin.

Paul's instructive emphasis in Romans 8 was, "You are a new person. You need not be controlled by the flesh. You are in the Spirit."

The Spirit quickens our bodies. We don't have to sin. We can live supernaturally. Our insecurities can evolve into feelings of adequacy and security. Resentments disappear. Fears become less and Christ's confidence in us reigns. Worry becomes trust and faith. As we know who we are, the result is abundant life. Knowing who we are comes through daily Bible study, the Holy Spirit's teaching, reminding oneself throughout the day and yielding to him.

"However," Paul might continue, "you can choose to ignore or forget about who you really are. You can walk after the flesh and reap death." The choice, moment by moment, is ours.

Do we know who we really are? Or, have we been living by the flesh so long that defeat and despair are our only expectations? We look forward to the next church revival, get pumped up for a while, but "reality" will strike sooner or later. Down we go.

What a contrast to the challenge in Romans 5 to "reign like kings"!

Yes, we have a "flesh," and there is Satan, both of which

would lead us to destruction. We must say "no" to both. But it is so much easier to say "no" if we are saturating our minds with new-creation thinking.

To understand how this works, we should return to an example used earlier. Through the eye gate, a woman sees her husband being too friendly with the neighbor lady. Thinking he might be involved with her, the wife reacts. Emotions come, such as fear, anger, jealousy. If they are allowed to remain, volcanic implosions or explosions could occur.

However, the new creation has another choice. "Just a minute," she might say, "I'm not thinking and acting like the person I really am. Fear, anger, jealousy are of the flesh. No, that's a part of the self-life that was cared for on the cross. If the Holy Spirit is in control, I can crucify these evil thoughts.

"Flesh no longer has control over me. In my new creation I am secure and adequate. I am complete in Christ. I don't need my husband's approval. I'm approved of by God. Even if my husband leaves me, God promises to work all to my good. Christ living in me gives me the desire and ability to forgive, love, and accept my husband just as he is. In fact, as I allow Christ to do so, he actually does the forgiving and loving through me."

What happens to anger, fear, and jealousy and their hurtful by-products? They go away. There is no implosion or explosion. The root cause, self, has been dealt with.

"Do I just let my husband walk all over me and not say anything to him?" the woman may ask. For his protection, and to improve her marriage, she should lovingly tell him the way she interpreted what she saw. But if she finds herself still angry, she shouldn't talk to him. For greatest results within and between the two of them, she should work on her attitude first.

Though she may say the right words, she still may be hanging on to anger, the expectation of his having eyes only for her. She may more honestly pray: "Father, I know I'm not behaving like the person I really am. At this point, I'd rather not let go of my expectation and anger. I'd like to pamper my flesh. Father, make this attitude repulsive to me. Soften my heart. Break my stubbornness."

At times the pain caused by pent-up anger will drive her to let go of the flesh. "All right, I've had enough pain. Father, I give you the expectation of my husband's having eyes only for me. You promise to meet all my needs, so I look only to you. Forgive and love my husband through me. And I'll look for a way to express love to him."

God would like to draw her with his love. "Jane, you're missing out on peace, joy, and fellowship with me. Hanging on to that flesh gives you no benefit but provides only some temporary get-even pleasure. Vengeance is mine; I will repay. Yield to who you are in me. Give me that burden, that bitterness, and you'll be at peace again."

THE DIVINE EXCHANGE—A PROCESS

Man enters life geared to be self-centered, which results in all kinds of self-destruction, including negative self-esteem. There is no responsiveness to God. Self, Satan, and the world value system control his thinking and behavior.

A divine exchange can take place. God draws the person to himself. Man receives the gift of salvation. There is a rebirth—a new creation. God's Spirit indwells the new creation, giving direction and power to live life abundantly, to reign as a king. Defeat need not take place.

However, there is a catch. Within this new creation there remain a body and soul that contain years of habit patterns of pride, insecurity, anger, and self-centeredness. Habit patterns don't change overnight.

Bad thought patterns surface in the new creation. "I want my way. What will they think of me? You've hurt me, so I'll get even. I'm not adequate. What's going to happen to us if the economy worsens?" And on and on.

What has happened here? Either (1) the person doesn't realize who he is as a new creation, so ignorance keeps him walking in the flesh, in destructive thought patterns; or (2) he forgets. New-creation thinking hasn't replaced negative thinking habits; or (3) there is rebellion. "I know who I am, but at this moment I want to think and act like a non-Christian."

There is such a thing as momentary unbelief in God. In seeking to gratify a desire or meet a need we may give in to old-nature thinking, desires of the body or sensual appetite. We, at that moment, believe Satan rather than God. Satan says, "You need this to make you happy," or "Look what he did to you. Get even with him."

At such times, we are not thinking and acting like who we really are. Consequently we miss out on God's peace, joy, and strength.

Inadequacy feelings should have no more control of us. Christ living through us provides our adequacy. We are dead to hurt and resentment. Christ is forgiving and loving through us.

As we apply these concepts, we develop a "Christ living through us" adequacy consciousness rather than the old "I'm no good" focus.

"But I've tried that, Dr. Burwick. It doesn't work," a middle-aged man said, telling how, after considerable study of new-creation material, the concepts didn't work for him.

"I die to myself. I confess sin. I remind myself who I am in Christ, but I still get so tense and fearful I strongly consider suicide."

I told Jim I was convinced God didn't want him to experience such stress. I read to him Paul's words to Timothy: "For God hath not given us the spirit of fear; but of power, and of love, and of a sound mind" (2 Timothy 1:7, KJV). Together we examined some possible hang-ups from the explanation given by Paul in Romans 6: to know (6:6); to reckon (6:11); to yield (6:13); and to obey (6:16).

To know. The first item Jim needed to review was what Paul said Christians are to know: "Knowing this, that our old man is crucified with him, that the body of sin might be destroyed, that henceforth we should not serve sin" (6:6).

I asked him if he was studying Romans 6—8, Ephesians 1—3, Colossians 1—3, Philippians 2—4, and the other passages emphasizing knowing God and knowing who he was in Christ. I had also given him other materials dealing with new-creation thinking.

"Well, Doc," Jim replied, "I'm so busy mornings that my personal time with God is rather sporadic. Most mornings I get ten to fifteen minutes of study and prayer. It's probably not enough."

"You're right," I answered. "With the tremendously distorted self-image we have, we need much more time getting to know God each morning. If we don't spend quality time and quantity time with him, we don't know who we are. Consequently, we don't know what resources we have."

I presented other "knowing" concepts to Jim. Not only are we to know positively who we are in relationship to God, but also negatively. We must be brutally honest with ourselves not to mask anger, impatience, fear, guilt, or other attributes of the flesh. We must face them and allow God to remove them.

Freedom that comes from knowing God is often stifled because the person unknowingly wants to hang onto some ingredient of the flesh, such as resentment. "The heart is deceitful. . . . desperately wicked. . . ."

The statement that I hear frequently in the counseling office is "Since being saved, I don't get angry." This person doesn't really know himself, because everyone gets angry.

Memorizing all the Bible won't help this person. Buried resentment can stop the new-creation freedom.

I usually ask people to write out their hurts, resentments, and guilts. This can help the individual to see them more plainly and to be repulsed by them. If we don't see the rottenness of the self-life we coddle it, and are never free from it. It contaminates the new creation and some kind of dysfunction occurs.

So, number one on the checklist is *to know* God our Father and how much he wants to do for us and through us, to know the rottenness of our flesh so that we can let it go. Such knowledge is a prerequisite for knowing who we really are in Christ, for knowing

God's standards and following them, rather than adhering to man's traditions, guidelines, and rules.

We study God's Word to know him better, to see our resources in him, and to see who we are in Christ.

Reckon. "To reckon" means "to accept something as certain." "Likewise reckon ye also yourselves to be dead indeed unto sin, but alive unto God through Jesus Christ our Lord" (Romans 6:11, KJV).

Jim had admitted that part of the reason for his acute fear and anxiety was his lack of "knowing," his failure to spend time with God daily.

The formal prayer time is spent with him, but it doesn't always affect the rest of the day. When in battle, the way we reckon or remind ourselves about what we know to be true about ourselves determines the outcome. It may be second nature to live by the facts that we know of ourselves, or we may have a tendency to live by feelings.

Jim, like so many of us, had to admit that when he felt fine, things went better. If he was tired, fearful, hurt, or worried, those bad feelings became his natural focus. Instead of basing his thinking on the facts of his new creation, he would let negative feelings control him, or slip back into old negative thought patterns developed before he became a Christian.

We must *know* God, our resource. We must remind ourselves, we must *reckon*, throughout the day about our resources in him.

Yield. The third key word is self-explanatory. "Neither yield ye your members as instruments of unrighteousness unto sin: but yield yourselves unto God, as those that are alive from the dead, and your members as instruments of righteousness unto God" (Romans 6:13, KJV).

Jim needed to learn consistency if he wanted ever to be effective. He tended to live by his feelings, which definitely leads to a yo-yo life-style. I knew we hadn't yet hit pay dirt in solving his problems.

I began to wonder if there was something blocking his total commitment to God, if there was some area in his life that was not yielded. God couldn't give total peace when there was anything being held back.

Jim and I began to probe pockets of resistance. I asked him, "Do you have expectations outside of God that aren't being met? Are you expecting your wife and children to treat you a certain way? Are they letting you down, causing hurt or resentment?" If true, those things had to be yielded. Our only expectation must be from God, who wants to meet all our needs. He may use our wives or husbands or children to meet the needs, but that is not to be our expectation. Desire—yes. Expectation—no.

"How about false gods, Jim? Are there any financial problems really bothering you, or fear of losing your position? If your trust is in money or a secure vocation, that must be yielded." God is our resource, not our money or our work.

I told Jim that a friend of mine had only one pocket of resistance that I could find, and that was pornographic magazines. He would not give up the erotic pleasure of ungodly sexual stimulation. I asked if anything like that was applicable in his situation.

I asked about his reputation. Lee LeFebre of Grace Fellowship asks his people, "Are you willing to endure humiliation potentially involved in coming to the end of yourself or in identifying with Christ?"

Jim's eyes lit up. "I don't want to fail. I don't want to face the humiliation of falling apart in front of my colleagues. My reputation is one of strength and capability. I don't ever want to appear weak."

Jim's insecurity was showing. He had done well in his profession, partly because he was capable and partly to prove to himself and others that he was an adequate person.

God was asking him to yield this area. Jim's greatest strength was as peanuts in God's economy. God was asking Jim to allow him to live supernaturally through him. Jim was fearful of the unknown, fearful of failure, fearful of loss of personality and reputation. He didn't believe that God would keep his word to meet all his needs.

This pocket of resistance appeared to be the cause for the

anxiety and mental confusion Jim was encountering. His commitment became: "Lord, I desire not to fail. I don't want to fall apart. I don't want to be viewed as incompetent; nevertheless, not my will but thine."

As Jim applied this "self-talk" throughout the days that followed, a real peace of mind took over. Jim later found that God even asked him to give up a good night's sleep. Before, when Jim would encounter insomnia, he would pop a sleeping pill. "If I didn't, I wouldn't be able to function the next day in my work. I'd lie there for a few hours, unable to go to sleep. I'd confess all my sins, remind myself who I was, but just couldn't hit slumberland."

Jim lay there, getting angry at God for not giving him sleep. His anger caused more sleeplessness. However, Jim began to pray, "Lord, I'm yielded to you. If you want me to go through the whole night without a wink of sleep, that's OK. You'll have to be my strength for tomorrow. I'm yours. You're in me, so sleep through me or stay awake through me—it's your choice."

Peace came. This man, who had previously been diagnosed as needing shock therapy, was finally free.

Obey. The last word in the barometer of measuring spiritual and emotional dysfunction is "obey." "Don't you realize that you can choose your own master? You can choose sin (with death) or else obedience (with acquittal). The one to whom you offer yourself—he will take you and be your master and you will be his slave" (Romans 6:16).

So often when people are saved and first become involved in the church, they are encouraged to obey all the church's and Bible's standards. "Do this. Don't do that. Be in church regularly. Get involved in witnessing programs, Bible study groups, and missionary societies." All of these activities are good, but the emphasis for the young believer should be on knowing God, the resource. With that knowledge as a basis, he allows God to live through him, instead of engaging in a lot of fleshly activity that often causes him to end as a burn-out or a drop-out. It is so much easier to obey when we know the resource with which to find strength to obey.

The Scripture is filled with promises about obediences. "Obey me and I will bless you," God's Word says repeatedly. If a person detects something wrong in his life, he should check his obedience. Is he tithing, giving thanks in all things, praising God no matter what the circumstances, spending time with God daily, studying, meditating, and praying, joyfully sharing of his means with others, being responsible in work and family life, keeping his body a fit temple of the Holy Spirit through proper, well-balanced diet and exercise?

A final way to function better is to resist Satan. Satan tempts us where we are weak. Most of us are not tempted to rob banks, but insecurity can provide Satan a foothold. He can increase our feelings of intimidation, our fears, our concerns for our protection.

Consequently, there are times in which our yielding to who we are in Christ must also include our direct command to flee Satan, for whom we are no match in our own strength. He has no real power over us, however, except as we allow him. Scripture is plain. "Resist the devil and he will flee from you."

PERSONAL APPLICATION

We must know who we are. We are not the inadequate, bumbling, resentful, guilt-ridden, fearful individuals we have been allowing Satan to make us think we still are.

We are new creations, born again, forgiven of all our sins, and washed in the blood of Jesus. We are the temple of the Holy Spirit, redeemed from the curse of the law, delivered from the power of darkness, and translated into God's kingdom. We are blessed, saints, holy and without blame before God, elect, victorious, set free, strong in the Lord. We are dead to sin, more than conquerors, complete in him, crucified and resurrected with Christ, joint heirs with Christ, chosen by God, accepted in the beloved.

As we know these things and remind ourselves of them throughout the day, and yield to who we are, we are free. If we don't, we will be in some kind of bondage.

We ought to set aside thirty to sixty minutes each early morning. First, we should ask God to show us any self-life we may be carrying that would thwart his teaching us about our real selves— our real identity.

If there is any resentment, worry, lust, or anything else which surfaces, we should confess it, repent of it, and turn away from it. Nothing must contaminate our minds if we are to plumb the depths of new-creation thinking.

Then we should ask God to teach us about our real identity. We might begin by studying the Scripture passages mentioned earlier in the chapter. Then we should study three or four of the "identity" verses at the end of this chapter. It would be best to read the whole chapter in which the verse appears. If a verse speaks specially to us, we should write it out on a three-by-five card and carry it with us for memorizing.

We should spend time daily in prayer, meditating on the concepts God is showing us. Then we should seek his wisdom to put those concepts in action for the day.

"He is my sufficiency for that meeting we have this noon," we might tell ourselves. He is our ability to forgive our husbands today, to love them, to do the things we know they appreciate most. Jesus, living in us, is our adequacy for the job challenge this morning.

How do we know ourselves? First, we saturate ourselves daily with the Word of God, especially the concepts of our identity in Christ as shown in the Scriptures at the end of this chapter.

To know ourselves we become sensitive to the Holy Spirit's convicting us of expressions of the "self-life." We must be quick to recognize attitudinal sins such as pride, anger, worry, lust, greed, and a critical spirit. There must be a corresponding quick and thorough repentance.

To know ourselves we walk in a way that matches our talk. We must allow Christ to live through us, to love others, to witness, to put others before ourselves. We must also be aware that there is a fleshly part of us that, if allowed to have control, will be harsh, critical, negative, angry, insecure, perfectionistic, workaholic, lustful, greedy, and self-centered.

When flesh rears its head, we can say, "No, that's not the real me." Satan tried three times to tempt Christ before his ministry began. After his forty-day fast in the wilderness, Christ was approached by Satan, who tempted him twice in regard to his identity: "If you are . . . turn the stone to bread." Later, "If you are . . . jump off the temple." And Satan continues to question our identity as well.

We begin to look at our circumstances. "Well," we say, "I would like to be a more thoughtful person, but my spouse gets downright rude." There is always the temptation to get angry and selfish and forget who we are. But God is our resource.

Who are we? The Bible says:

I am God's child, born again of the incorruptible seed *(1 Peter 1:23)*.

I am the salt of the earth *(Matthew 5:13)*.

I am the light of the world *(Matthew 5:14)*.

I am set free *(John 8:31-33)*.

I am his disciple because I have love for others *(John 13:34, 35)*.

I am protected by the power of his name *(John 17:11)*.

I am filled with joy *(John 17:3)*.

I am kept from the evil one *(John 17:15)*.

I am one with God the Father and Jesus the Son *(John 17:23)*.

I am God's gift to Christ *(John 17:24)*.

I am a saint *(Romans 1:7)*.

I am made right in God's sight by faith *(Romans 5:1)*.

I am at peace with God *(Romans 5:1)*.

I am in the place of highest privilege *(Romans 5:2)*.

I am confidently and joyfully looking forward to becoming all God has in mind for me *(Romans 5:2)*.

I am rejoicing in troubles, because through them God is building me up and making me strong *(Romans 5:3-5)*.

I am justified, and there is "much more" available to me *(Romans 5:9)*.

I am reconciled to God and awaiting his great blessing *(Romans 5:10)*.

I am now reigning as a king because of Jesus Christ within me *(Romans 5:17)*.

I am a receiver of God's grace that far supersedes my worst sin *(Romans 5:20)*.

I am dead to the old man; consequently, my flesh is powerless *(Romans 6:6)*.

I am dead to sin and alive to God in Christ Jesus *(Romans 6:11)*.

I am yielded to God. All my rights and expectations are his *(Romans 6:13)*.

I am a recipient of eternal life through Jesus Christ *(Romans 6:23)*.

I am rotten through and through if the flesh is in control *(Romans 6:18)*.

I am free from condemnation *(Romans 8:1)*.

I am freed from the vicious cycle of sin and death *(Romans 8:2)*.

I am following after the Holy Spirit which leads to life and peace *(Romans 8:6)*.

I am a son of God; consequently I am led by the Spirit of God *(Romans 8:14)*.

I am a son of God and joint-heir with Christ, sharing all his treasures *(Romans 8:17)*.

I am confident that all things work together for good *(Romans 8:28)*.

I am being conformed to the image of Christ *(Romans 8:29)*.

I have been given all things *(Romans 8:32)*.

I am protected. Who can ever be against me? *(Romans 8:31)*.

I am inseparable from God's love *(Romans 8:35)*.

I am more than a conqueror through Christ *(Romans 8:37)*.

I am established to the end *(1 Corinthians 1:8)*.

I am infused with Jesus, made acceptable to God, pure and holy *(1 Corinthians 1:30)*.

MY REAL IDENTITY

I am a recipient of things too wonderful even to imagine *(1 Corinthians 2:9)*.

I am God's temple, indwelt by the Holy Spirit (1 Corinthians 3:16, 17).

I am already full, rich, and I reign as a king *(1 Corinthians 4:8)*.

I am washed, sanctified, and justified in Jesus *(1 Corinthians 6:11)*.

I am of one spirit with God *(1 Corinthians 6:17)*.

I have been bought with a price *(1 Corinthians 6:20)*.

I am in the image and glory of God *(1 Corinthians 11:7)*.

I am always led about in Christ's triumphal procession *(2 Corinthians 2:14)*.

I am a sweet aroma manifesting the presence of God wherever I go *(2 Corinthians 2:14)*.

I am adequate for anything because my adequacy comes from God *(2 Corinthians 3:5)*.

I am a new creation, the old is past; new is coming *(2 Corinthians 5:17)*.

I am Christ's ambassador *(2 Corinthians 5:20)*.

I am strongest when I am weakest *(2 Corinthians 12:10)*.

I am crucified and the life I now live is not mine but Christ's *(Galatians 2:20)*.

I am redeemed from the curse of the law *(Galatians 3:13)*.

I am filled with the fruit of the spirit: love, joy, peace, etc. *(Galatians 5:22, 23)*.

I am in Christ Jesus *(Ephesians 1:1)*.

I am blessed with every spiritual blessing *(Ephesians 1:3)*.

I am chosen by God to be holy and blameless *(Ephesians 1:4)*.

I am predestined for adoption as a son through Jesus *(Ephesians 1:5)*.

I am accepted in the beloved *(Ephesians 1:6)*.

I am forgiven all my sins *(Ephesians 1:7)*.

I am lavished with his wisdom and insight to know his will *(Ephesians 1:8, 9)*.

I am predestined according to his purpose *(Ephesians 1:11)*.

I am made alive with Christ *(Ephesians 2:1, 5)*.

I am raised with Christ and seated in heavenly places *(Ephesians 2:6)*.

I have been saved by faith through God's gift of grace *(Ephesians 2:8)*.

I am God's handiwork, created in Christ unto good works *(Ephesians 2:10)*.

I am a fellow citizen with the saints, God's household *(Ephesians 2:19)*.

I am built upon the foundation of the apostles, prophets, and Christ, the cornerstone *(Ephesians 2:20)*.

I am able to walk boldly into God's presence *(Ephesians 3:12)*.

I am strengthened with power through his Spirit in the inner man *(Ephesians 3:16)*.

I am indwelt with Christ to know the fullness of his love *(Ephesians 3:17-19)*.

I am receiving exceeding abundantly above all that I ask or think *(Ephesians 3:20)*.

I am walking worthily because of all the insights of Ephesians 1—3 *(Ephesians 4:1)*.

I am becoming mature, the measure of the stature of the fullness of Christ *(Ephesians 4:13)*.

I am no longer a child but growing up in all aspects of Christ *(Ephesians 4:14, 15)*.

I am laying aside the old self, renewing my mind for living a life of holiness and righteousness *(Ephesians 4:22, 24)*.

I am laying aside lies, anger, stealing, unwholesome communication *(Ephesians 4:25-31)*.

I am kind, tenderhearted, and forgiving *(Ephesians 4:32)*.

I am strong in the Lord to fight off all Satan's attacks *(Ephesians 6:10-17)*.

I am confident of his finishing the work in me unto perfection *(Philippians 1:6)*.

I am a citizen of heaven *(Philippians 3:20)*.

I am rejoicing in the Lord always *(Philippians 4:4)*.

I am anxious for nothing *(Philippians 4:6)*.

I am guarded by God's peace; my mind has no turmoil *(Philippians 4:7)*.

I am able to do all things through Christ who strengthens me *(Philippians 4:13)*.

I am having all my needs met according to his riches *(Philippians 4:19)*.

I am filled with the knowledge of his will in all wisdom and understanding *(Colossians 1:9)*.

I am able to walk worthy of the Lord, fully pleasing him, being fruitful *(Colossians 1:10)*.

I am strengthened with all power according to his might unto all patience and joy *(Colossians 1:11)*.

I have been delivered from the domain of darkness and transferred to the kingdom of God *(Colossians 1:13)*.

I am indwelt by him in whom all fullness dwells *(Colossians 1:19)*.

I have been presented to God—holy, blameless, and beyond reproach *(Colossians 1:22)*.

I am filled with God's power that works mightily in me *(Colossians 1:29)*.

I am complete in Christ, filled with God, possessor of everything *(Colossians 2:10)*.

I am blameless *(Colossians 2:12-15)*.

I am growing because my nourishment and strength come from God *(Colossians 2:19)*.

I am being renewed to a true knowledge according to the image of Jesus *(Colossians 3:10)*.

I am chosen *(1 Thessalonians 1:4)*.

I am not given a spirit of fear, but of power, and of love, and a sound mind *(2 Timothy 1:7)*.

I am adequate, complete, equipped for every good work *(2 Timothy 3:17)*.

I am delivered from every evil deed and will be brought safely to his kingdom *(2 Timothy 4:18)*.

I am able to come boldly before the throne of grace to find mercy and grace *(Hebrews 4:16)*.

I am confident that he will never leave me and I fear not what men can do to me *(Hebrews 13:5, 6)*.

I am lacking no wisdom *(James 1:5)*.

I am kept by the power of God *(1 Peter 1:5)*.

I am loved, and have been washed from my sins by his blood *(Revelation 1:5)*.

I am victorious *(Revelation 21:7)*.

EIGHT

A PRICE TO PAY

 **Someone** has said, "Every broken thing is but the assurance that God is making something." "We see broken things as tragedies and we cast them aside as junk. But God sees broken things as opportunity for his glory and casts unbroken things away as useless."

Jesus took a boy's lunch of bread and fish, broke it and blessed it, and it fed five thousand. Gideon and his three hundred men broke pitchers, causing such a diffusion of light that their enemies were frightened into defeat.

The box of precious ointment that was brought to anoint Christ's feet had to be broken before perfume filled the house.

Jesus Christ's broken body on Golgotha's hill was the supreme example of brokenness that brought salvation and new life to whoever would receive him.

God is looking for broken men and women, not the proud, unbending, self-sufficient breed that fills our church pews. He seeks people who will cooperate in allowing him to bring them to the end of themselves so that they say, "It is not I that live, but Christ through me."

"Hold it, Burwick," certain psychologists say. "You're preaching 'worm theology.' Man was created beautiful and wonderful. You're saying he has to become nothing. We have too many Christians who see themselves as nothing and are living defeated lives."

In their quest for building positive self-esteem in the Christian community, such psychologists, in my opinion, have whitewashed the real message of the cross.

They are right in one sense, for many Christians do live defeated lives. However it is not because they focus on their nothingness.

They are defeated because they have masked their rottenness. The putrid stench seeps through the maze of masks, polluting Christlike, positive thought processes.

The people of a certain beautiful new office complex began to smell a rancid odor. Amidst the steel, brick, glass, and new paint, the pungent smell of garbage surfaced. After a little research was done, it was found that the building sat on a landfill of garbage.

How often this is true of Christians! We're so busy in all our Christian activity. We look so good. But the smell of garbage seeps through—harshness, stubbornness, unteachableness, pride, lust, resentment, fear, and worry. As the garbage lies rotting within, covered by a multitude of marks, our self-esteem continues to grow smaller, as a subconscious haunting voice yells from within: "Something's not right in here."

We pay no attention until there is a crisis. God uses business reversals, marriage and family conflicts, disease, depression, and a number of other discomforts to bring us to the end of ourselves —to brokenness—to where we say, "I can't go on living in my own strength. God must take over and produce through me what I am unable to do in my own strength."

The author of *Streams in the Desert* described it like this:

> How an old harper dotes on his harp! How he fondles and caresses it, as a child resting on his bosom! His life is bound up in it. But, see him tuning it. He grasps it firmly, strikes a chord with a sharp, quick blow; and while it quivers as if in pain, he leans over intently to catch the first note that rises. The note, as he feared, is false and harsh. He strains the chord with the torturing thumbscrew; and though it seems ready to snap with the tension, he strikes it again, bending down to listen softly as before, till at length you see a smile on his face as the first true tone trembles upward.
>
> So it may be that God is dealing with you, loving you better than any harper loves his harp. He finds you a mass of jarring discords. He wrings your heartstrings with some torturing anguish; He bends over you tenderly, striking and listening; and hearing only a harsh murmur, strikes you again, while His heart bleeds for you, anxiously waiting for that strain—"Not my will but Thine be done"—which is melody sweet to His ear as angels' songs. Nor will He cease to strike until your chastened soul shall blend with all the pure and infinite harmonies of His own being.

Our greatest sin as Christians is deceit, dishonesty with ourselves, covering sins of attitude. For God to live his supernatural life through us, our vessels must be clean and empty, responding positively to the wringing and plucking of our heavenly harper. In John 15, Jesus said, "Without me you can do nothing."

Breaking experiences bring us to the awareness of what is wrong within. As we repent and God shows us our inadequacy to live the abundant Christian life, our view of ourselves becomes: "We're clean, empty of self, a temple of the Holy Spirit in and through which the power of God can live."

"Now hold it, Burwick," someone might say. "It sounds as if you are talking about a spiritual schizophrenic. Is it your body and someone else living through you? Are you speaking of a spiritual R2D2, a puppet, a zombie?"

There are people in the mental wards of our hospitals who think they are God or the Messiah. I am not referring to this type of irrationality.

Jesus set the pattern for us in John, chapters 5, 6, and 7, in which it is recorded that he said, "I do nothing of myself, but only as the Father lives through me, do I live." Paul built upon this concept, "It is not I that live but Christ in me" (Galatians 2:20).

But before this can happen, there must be a brokenness of self-effort, self-confidence.

Paul spoke of Christians being filled with the Holy Spirit. It isn't possible for God to fill us with his Spirit when we are full of ourselves.

The extreme example of the self-life is depicted in the story of Peer Gynt, where people in an insane asylum are described: "It is here that men are most themselves. Themselves and nothing but themselves. Sailing with outspread sails of self. Each shuts himself in a cask of self. The cask is stopped with a bung of self ... seasoned in a well of self. None has a tear for others' woes, or cares about what any other thinks."

So many of us find ourselves in a mental institution of self: "If my circumstances would only change. If my wife would only change, I'd be OK." "If my husband would just spend some time with me I wouldn't be so depressed."

The world-renowned analyst Dr. Fritz Kunkel said, "It has been shown that all mistakes, weaknesses, and aberrations can be traced back to man's *egocentricity*—people wrapped too much in self. The fundamental problem of self-education is the problem of overcoming one's egocentricity."

An attorney friend of mine described his life: "I was really into positive thinking. I listened to all the right tapes and read the PMA (positive mental attitude) books. I made a lot of money, won a lot of lawsuits that I really shouldn't have won. I exuded such confidence that I could sway juries. But, Ray, what it did for me was to build a tremendous amount of self-confidence to the point that I felt the whole world revolved around me. I became a conceited, arrogant hot dog... until the Lord brought me into an impossible situation. I crashed. He got my attention and drew me to himself."

How do we empty ourselves of self to experience the supernatural living the Bible says is available to us? Often I hear Christians say, "But I've confessed it." They don't realize that confession resolves the sin, but doesn't change the sinner—the egocentricity.

Do we go on long fasts, sell all we have and wear rags to empty ourselves of self? Do we become missionaries or give up all possessions to become filled with the Spirit? These aren't the answer.

On June 12, 1973, I was sitting in the waiting room of the obstetrics section of Sacred Heart Hospital in Spokane, Washington.

One young prospective father was handling his tension by chain smoking. Another man was talking nonstop. Ann and I were expecting twins, and I was overwhelmed with anticipation.

We were, of course, destined to have two strong healthy boys to match the two beautiful girls we already had. I could picture them sixteen years later, playing ball together, singing together, praying and preaching together.

A PRICE TO PAY

My fantasy was interrupted by our pediatrician. "Well, Ray, you've got a strong, healthy boy."

"What about the other one, Doc?"

"You mean they haven't told you?" Neither the obstetrician nor the nurse had informed me of the birth.

"No, what should they have told me?"

"I'm sorry, Ray, your other boy was stillborn."

Oh, the hurt! The joy of having one healthy boy was so exhilarating, yet there was sorrow over the death of the other boy. What confusion! What tearing! On the one hand, thanking God, and on the other, questioning him. On the one hand, blessing, and on the other hand, hurt, anger, and sorrow.

I asked a nurse for a piece of paper and a pen. I feared bottling any negative emotion which would have complicated matters. I wrote, wept, prayed. I shook my fist at God. I praised God. Oh, the pain!

I left the hospital and went home to the place where Ann and I had seen our marriage falling apart. This death seemed to be the final blow of several months of deep pain.

Ann had gone through a severe emotional trauma months before. She and I had nearly destroyed each other with our bitterness towards each other. Divorce seemed to be the only way out. Then came the pregnancy, totally unplanned. Months of pregnancy problems put her in bed.

I often had to rush her to the emergency room because of complications. Then . . . this child's death.

I sat alone in that large, quiet, six-bedroom frame house that night. The great athlete, the super coach, the effective counselor —broken. The bright lights of the coliseums were out. The cheering fans were gone, and all that had been accomplished seemed as wood, hay, and stubble.

"Now, Lord, why? Why all this to a guy who for twenty-seven years has been dedicated to you, has given you his life, has sought you to be first in everything he did. Why, Lord?"

The confident Ray Burwick who could "do anything" was

This is the birth announcement that our daughters designed. It was posted in the OB ward for months and ministered to many people. (Amy and Gretchen were five and six at the time.)

IT WAS NIP AND TUCK FOR MOMMY FOR 8 MONTHS...

HE GAVE US TUCK WHO IS 5LBS. 15OZ. 18¾" RAY OLAF BURWICK II MOMMY AND BABY ARE DOING GREAT!

THANK YOU JESUS!

ON JUNE 12TH. JESUS DECIDED TO KEEP NIP WHO WE NAMED JAY OLIVER

broken. The marriage was a mess. A dead child. What else matters?

"Every broken thing is but the assurance that God is making something. We see broken things as tragedies and we cast them aside as junk. But God sees broken things as opportunity for his glory and casts unbroken things away as useless."

A strong, growing Christian bears the marks and scars of failures, of disappointments, and humility. Scripture is replete with examples: Joseph, Paul, Moses, Abraham, Elijah, all broken, but raised to greatness.

It's as if our loving heavenly Father is saying to us: "I have something greater for you. Remember, in Romans 5 repeatedly Paul said 'much more' is available to you. I love you the way you are, and I am expressing myself through you in very wonderful ways now; but I would like to bless you even more. So let me strip you more of self.

"Self-effort, self-confidence will be replaced by my power. Relax. Go through this breaking time with me and you'll even be stronger when it's finished."

Jesus said, "This is my body, broken for you." The ultimate brokenness—Jesus broken for my salvation, for my eternal life with him, for my peace and joy now. Thank you, Jesus.

When our world crashes and we come to an absolute end, we penetrate the depths of true searching, listening, worship and growth. Awareness of God is most vivid at such times. Awareness of self and circumstances diminishes because the pain is too great. The only way out is to look up. What insight we can gather from the promises of Scripture:

> Let everyone bless God and sing his praises, for he holds our lives in his hands. And he holds our feet to the path. You have purified us with fire, O Lord, like silver in a crucible. You captured us in your net and laid great burdens on our backs. You sent troops to ride across our broken bodies. We went through fire and flood. But in the end, you brought us into wealth and great abundance (Psalm 66:8-12).

> God is our refuge and strength, a tested help in times of trouble. And

so we need not fear even if the world blows up, and the mountains crumble into the sea (Psalm 46:1, 2).

I waited patiently for God to help me; then he listened and heard my cry. He lifted me out of the pit of despair, out from the bog and the mire, and set my feet on a hard, firm path and .... has given me a new song to sing, of praises to our God. Now many will hear of the glorious things he did for me, and stand in awe before the Lord, and put their trust in him. Many blessings are given to those who trust the Lord, and have no confidence in those who are proud, or who trust in idols (Psalm 40:1-4).

Nuggets of this size escape us in our frantic self-life efforts.

At times, God hits our pocketbooks to get our attention. He may ruin us to bless us. The rich young ruler came to Christ and said, "What must I do to get eternal life?"

We see Jesus' response: " 'If you want to be perfect, go and sell everything you have and give the money to the poor, and you will have treasure in heaven; and come, follow me.' But when the young man heard this, he went away sadly, for he was very rich" (Matthew 19:21, 22).

Does the Lord have our bank accounts? Are we so broken before him, that if he says to us "Sell and follow me," we will be quick to comply? For the Creator to live through us supernaturally, producing greatest self-esteem, we must not be hanging onto anything that would come between him and us.

"Are you telling me it's wrong to be rich, Burwick?"

"Yes, if wealth thwarts God's work in your life." Jesus challenged us, "Anyone who gives up his home, brothers, sisters, father, mother, children, or property, to follow me, shall receive a hundred times as much in return, and shall have eternal life" (Matthew 19:29).

When the Lord called us to full-time missionary work in 1968, we had to leave brothers, homes, sisters, father, mother, children, and property. But it has been exciting to see that, even though he stripped us of everything, down to just a sack of flour in the kitchen, he has given us one hundred times as many brothers, sisters, fathers, and mothers as when we lived in California, Oklahoma, Washington, Idaho, and now Alabama. He has multiplied loved ones to us many times. The only thing that he hasn't multiplied one hundredfold is property, and I've been talking to him about that. "Lord, what's the problem?"

God seems to be saying, "Ray, when I can trust you with it, I'll give it to you."

Broken? "Yes, Lord. You are my Resource. I tend to look at my work, my ability to produce as a money-maker. You say you want to be my Resource. I trust you. When you know I can handle your blessing or riches, you'll take from me the present blessing of tight finances. Thank you, Jesus!"

My real treasure, dwelling within me, is Christ. In him I have all things. In him there is not the slightest lack in purity or power. He longs not only to fill my life with his gracious Spirit but to overflow through me, producing victorious living and a positive self-image.

But my hard shell of unbroken humanity holds back this flow of life. The reason that Christ is not seen so much today is that there is not much brokenness in Christ's people.

In T. A. Haggar's words, "God must have broken vessels. Unbrokenness hides our treasure ... the Lord Jesus Christ, only brokenness reveals him."

Can I trust God for my circumstances realizing he is in the process of breaking me from self-centeredness, out of which will develop a God-centeredness producing the ultimate in positive self-esteem?

Jesus said, "If you insist on saving your life, you will lose it. Only those who throw away their lives for my sake and for the sake of the Good News will ever know what it means to really live" (Mark 8:35).

George Mueller was the first "franchiser of orphanages," and raising millions of dollars to build and support many orphanages, not by a well organized PR program, but simply by prayer.

To one who asked the secret of his service, George Mueller said, "There was a day when I died. Utterly died." As he spoke he bent lower until he almost reached the floor and he added, "I died to George Mueller, his opinions, his preferences, his tastes and will. I died to the world, its approval or its censure. I died to the approval or blame of even my brethren and my friends. Since then I have studied only to show myself approved unto God."

Some believe that the view of the crucified life is degrading to both God and to man. They claim that in one instance we are told to become worms for Jesus and in another we are told to bring our lives to death. These views, they say, are degrading to man because we become subhuman, worthless, hollow shells rather than free, creative personalities who respond to God and love.

Such people have a hard time relating to John 15:5 (KJV): "Without me ye can do nothing." The Pauline concept "In me (that is, in my flesh,) dwelleth no good thing" (Romans 7:17) is foreign to the person who has sufficient ego strength to function on his own.

Most Christians don't like to admit to the rottenness within. Pride, lust, self-reliance and anger are often masked by religious fervor or self-confidence. Instead of facing self for what it really is, and its hindrance of the power of God working through us, we mask it. We gloss it over. We don't see the rottenness, or smell its stench prompting us to resolve it biblically. Consequently, those Christians never experience the supernatural life promised to them.

Obviously, we can get stuck in the rottenness concept and focus on death to self. Some Christians become obsessed with "I died with Christ." Death is just the first step. But it does provide hope.

I don't have to be controlled by my insecurities, which was part of the reason for my stuttering. I don't have to be dominated by it. It is part of the old man, part of the man that died with Christ. As I stand shaking in my boots while speaking before a large crowd, I can say, "Hold it. That insecurity died with you, Lord. It is part of the ugly self that does not have to control me any longer. And because of that death with you, Lord, the power of your Holy Spirit can live through me, talk through me, and talk to me as I talk. Thank you, Lord."

What impact this has in building positive self-esteem! The

broken life is aware of the keen balance between honesty with the flesh when it asserts itself, taking it to the cross, repenting of the sin, and leaving it there, and refocusing on new-creation thinking. The ultimate in brokenness keeps in our mind the truth that "I am holy, a saint, forgiving, loving, patient, and that I can do all things through Christ...."

Someone described the clean and empty state of brokenness like this: "I have become, as it were, wind chimes, awaiting God's breath to sing to passersby any melody he chooses."

Some of us are in that growth stage of passiveness right now. We have been so performance oriented, so self-confident and self-reliant that God has to give us a "Moses at the back of the desert" experience. He must strip us of self-effort, so we find a passive, almost rocking chair setting—wind chimes, awaiting God's breath to sing to passersby any melody he chooses.

"Lord, I don't know what is going on," we may say. "I feel that you are stripping me. Doors are closed. I can't do anything. You are breaking me. I'd like to run. I'd like to get into some activity. But I'll wait, and rest, and see what you are doing in my life.

"Then, Lord, you begin to open up doors when you see I'm ready. When it is right, Lord, it will be you and me, charging ahead. Right now I'll wait. Lord, I trust you."

This is the passive step—the wind chimes experience God takes certain people through. The workaholic must learn to rest and operate in the power of God's might. The hard-driving person must be mellowed to experience God's peace.

However, this is usually not a stage that lazy, undisciplined folks go through. In counseling, I have had this kind of person use this argument for being passive as a justification for laziness. "I don't have to face responsibility," they say. "I'll just sit back and allow the Lord to do it all!" This person needs to understand Paul's statement: "Stay away from any Christian who spends his days in laziness and does not follow the ideal of hard work" (2 Thessalonians 3:6). Anyone who is lazy doesn't qualify as wind chimes.

Possibly some of us are at a growth stage where God is asking us to dream an impossible dream. We should set goals so high that their accomplishment can only be accredited to God.

Robert Schuller, whose dynamic goal setting and possibility thinking built the cathedral of glass in California, spoke of Jesus this way: "Jesus wanted to draw all men to himself. But the cross sanctifies the self-esteem from what would otherwise turn out to be dangerous, ruthless pride."

What is the difference between dangerous egotism and wholesome divine self-esteem? Schuller says, "The difference is the cross you are willing to bear to fulfill God's will. Before God can give you the crown, the grand and glorious redemptive holy pride, he will purge you and make your self-esteem sanctified and sacred. There is no success without a cross."

Paul wrote of these breaking situations:

> But all these things that I once thought very worthwhile—now I've thrown them all away so that I can put my trust and hope in Christ alone. Yes, everything else is worthless when compared with the priceless gain of knowing Christ Jesus my Lord. I have put aside all else, counting it worth less than nothing, in order that I can have Christ, and become one with him, no longer counting on being saved by being good enough or by obeying God's laws, but by trusting in Christ to save me; for God's way of making us right with himself depends on faith— counting on Christ alone. Now I have given up everything else—I have found it to be the only way to really know Christ and to experience the mighty power that brought him back to life again, and to find out what it means to suffer and to die with him. So, whatever it takes, I will be one who lives in the fresh newness of life of those who are alive from the dead (Philippians 3:7-11).

As you and I see our death in Christ, we can then expect the fresh awareness of his life to permeate us. And so often that awareness comes through brokenness, divorce, separation, business reversals, child-rearing traumas, and death.

Often we look at these experiences negatively. We must view these hurts as Paul did: "Therefore, I am well content with weaknesses, with insults, with distresses, with persecutions, with difficulties, for Christ's sake; for whem I am weak, then I am strong (2 Corinthians 10:10, NASB).

Suffering purifies personalities, builds character qualities, and conforms to his image those who submit trustingly to God's pruning tool. Brokenness leads to power.

I am thankful that we don't have to jack ourselves up every morning, saying, "I'm OK and you're OK." I'm glad we can awaken each morning not being controlled by our feelings or our circumstances.

PERSONAL APPLICATION

No one of stable mind enjoys pain. In fact, many people are too quick to relieve pain through alcohol, drugs, and other escapes.

Obviously, the pain of arthritis, an extracted tooth, or cancer can and should be relieved. Medication is certainly in order. However, our pleasure-seeking society needs to reexamine suffering and find that it can produce great benefits.

We need to study suffering. The following is a skeleton outline to help us see the benefits and reasons for suffering (brokenness) in building positive self-esteem.

1. Our fallen nature (self-life) causes suffering (Ephesians 2:3).
   a. Consequently, we hurt (Romans 8:22, 23).
   b. Consequently, we hurt others.
2. Satan causes suffering (Job; Luke 13:16; 1 Corinthians 5:5; 1 Timothy 1:20; 1 Peter 5:8, 9).
3. There are natural discomforts that all suffer for which God comforts us so that we can comfort others (2 Corinthians 1:3-7).
4. Some suffering is discipline (punishment) for sin, leading to growth of character (Hebrews 12:5-11; Isaiah 1:25, NASB).
5. Some suffering is faith being tested, our dross refined (1 Peter 1:7; Job 23:10).
6. Some suffering is for crushing, as in perfume making, to influence others to Christ (2 Corinthians 2:14-16).

7. God uses suffering to build patience and growth in character, strength (Romans 5:3-5; James 1:2-4).

8. Suffering is a natural by-product of sin (Psalm 53; Psalm 38:3-8; Deuteronomy 28—30).

9. Suffering comes from the sins of our parents (Numbers 14:18).

10. As a grain of wheat dies and bears thirty, sixty, and one hundredfold, so we, as we die to self, bear fruit (John 12:24).

11. God uses in a great way broken men, such as Moses, Paul, Joseph, Noah, and Peter.

12. God promises tribulation and affliction (John 16:33; Psalm 34:19).

13. Suffering silences Satan as it did in Job's case.

14. Suffering glorifies God. Jesus allowed Lazarus to die in order to raise him (John 11:4, 5).

15. Suffering is part of what conforms us to the image of Christ (Romans 8:28, 29; Hebrews 2:10; Philippians 3:10).

16. Suffering makes us appreciative.

17. Suffering can bring humility and obedience (2 Corinthians 12:7-10; Deuteronomy 8:2-5; Hebrews 5:7, 8).

18. Suffering teaches us to pray and to dig into Scripture for answers.

19. Suffering brings rewards (2 Timothy 2:12).

20. Suffering is a pathway to eternal glory and makes us partners with Christ to share in his glory (2 Corinthians 4:17, 18; Romans 8:17; 1 Peter 5:10; 1 Peter 4:12, 13).

21. When we are suffering, sin and evil desires lose their power over us (1 Peter 4:1, 2).

22. Sometimes we must choose—pleasure of sin or suffering affliction (Hebrews 11:25).

23. We are persecuted for righteousness' sake (Matthew 5:10, 12).

24. Suffering teaches us God's statutes, to keep us from going astray (Psalm 119:67, 71; Hebrews 5:8). When the Israelites prospered, they forsook God, they suffered, and then came back to God.

25. Suffering from self-giving leads to growth in *agape* love (Matthew 20:25-28; 1 Corinthians 13:4).
26. Suffering leads to faith building (Job 13:15, KJV).
27. We do not surrender self-will if all seems to be going well for us. Pain insists upon being attended to and is sometimes relieved only by surrender (2 Corinthians 7:8-10).

C. S. Lewis wrote in *The Problem of Pain* (New York: Macmillan, 1943):

> And pain is not only immediately recognisable evil, but evil impossible to ignore. We can rest contentedly in our sins and in our stupidities; and anyone who has watched gluttons shovelling down the most exquisite foods as if they did not know what they were eating, will admit that we can ignore even pleasure. But pain insists upon being attended to. God whispers to us in our pleasures, speaks in our conscience, but shouts in our pains: it is His megaphone to rouse a deaf world.

We must not be quick to escape pain through drugs, busyness, or other escape mechanisms. There is a place for medication and busyness, but we must make sure that if the pain is from heaven, we will receive the full benefit of it as we recognize its cause and properly deal with it.

Someone may ask, "If pain, suffering, and brokenness are so profitable, shouldn't we pursue them?"

In itself, suffering has no value. The results of suffering may be of value. Paul wrote: "[God] has showered down upon us the richness of his grace—for how well he understands us and knows what is best for us at all times" (Ephesians 1:8). Sometimes what is best for us is suffering and brokenness.

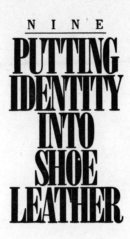

NINE

PUTTING IDENTITY INTO SHOE LEATHER

Walk with me through the challenging network of intricate, confusing pathways leading from distorted self-image to positive self-esteem.

A client of mine, Roy (not his real name), is allowing us to follow his walk. He is a very intelligent man in his mid-twenties. Roy holds a highly regarded executive position and has had a pattern of achievement throughout his school years.

Roy came to my office highly anxious and depressed. Clarifying his sexuality and building self-confidence were two other areas of his concern. He knew he wasn't homosexual, but his feelings toward some men were strangely conflicting to him.

To get a look at his inner workings, listen to what he wrote one Sunday afternoon:

It has been a bad afternoon, a panorama of sorrows has paraded through my stunned brain. I'm not responsible for this, but the helpless victim. And the parade is not unfamiliar—it is often restaged.

The parade's theme: my worthlessness and misery. Its characters: old familiar anxieties, enclosing me and pushing me back, breathless, against the restraining ropes.

When I am left alone, I am not nice to myself. I pommel myself, struggling and merciless. Weapons—all of them effective—are well-known and chosen for their effectiveness and familiarity.

I am exhausted, tired, scared, mad, lonesome, turbulent. I don't want to do anything.

There is a long held feeling that I am unworthy for any competition. I've proved it wrong, but haven't learned (relearned) the lesson.

Roy wrestled with these destructive thoughts periodically. They left him wiped out for days after. He continued to write:

The world must see me as a total fool, a failure. Again, I've proved differently; but, after time and with close inspection, I fear they will reach the dreaded conclusion. I lack a solid base on which to found myself. There is insufficient strength within myself—or at least my little strength merits such small amounts of self-respect that I dare not use it.

I wallow between love and hate, satisfaction and misery. Today, death would be better than any more of this. I am simply unable to defend myself against my enemy, myself.

Concerns: my abnormality. It's been severe and significant. My fears are confirmed, my spirits are low.

Why was I created this way? Why was I allowed to develop? Did no one see my abnormalities? Why wasn't I helped? Now, I fear, it's too late.

Everything is done for effect. What will others say or think? Will I be able to fool them again this time? Can I squeak by another time with my self-respect? Do I wear the right clothes, speak correct English, know the right people? Am I bright enough, interesting enough, erudite enough? Probably not. And I loathe the consequences.

I fear myself. I fear I am terribly bad, terribly odd, terribly loathsome.

Where did these fears originate? Why do they continue to chase me? Why do I give them credence? I do not have the choice in the matter.

On days like these, I am not myself. I am consumed by an evil, destructive force. I hurt, violently.

Is this a chemical reaction? Satanic? I know it is real, whatever the origin. And I pray for relief.

Spare me, O God, for my soul is in agony.

Roy described his childhood for us.

I didn't play football. I was too delicate—in everything. A mother's boy. A sissy? Not really, for I fought it. But I was always craving acceptance from my peers, especially males. And I rarely, if ever, got it. Even from my father. There was deep criticism and, I detected, shame. He had to tolerate me but he didn't have to like me. And he tried to change everything about me from the way I ate to the way I spoke. Even today he disapproves; only recently I was told my mannerisms were undesirable and that my choice of a girl friend didn't suit him.

I have wasted years and opportunities looking for—frantically seeking—his approval. I need him to say I am all right, not for him to begrudgingly acknowledge that a particular skill or accomplishment suits him. Those acknowledgements are most like anomalies—surprise which I surprise him with, shaking his negative image of me.

These roots must be the key to self-approval. I must seek them out and conquer them. I must return to the site and be healed.

PUTTING IDENTITY INTO SHOE LEATHER

It's no wonder, then, that I hurt when I see others dealing normally in their situations. For instance, Joe golfed with his father. He won his father's companionship and respect. And Jack, my own brother, grew up with the same set of rules, the same environment. Yet, he is unaffected. But I don't have to look far to see why. Jack was the accepted son. It was he who courted the business and sports interests. It was he who developed the father/son camaraderie. I was jettisoned, cast off to land where I would. In fact, I suspect I was sacrificed to be the daughter my mother never had. A friend says I was always the weapon he used to fight with my mother. And I'm not sure he likes her either.

I was the sensitive one during all of this, and still am the one who cried when animals got hurt (how could I kill one?), the one who would have offered my bed to Jesus had he come visiting. These sensitivities made my plight more hurtful.

Something happened. It was the fifth grade—I remember it well. Mrs. Massey and a classmate named Janet. The terrible assassins. They took my name, ganged up, excluded me. I became paranoid, lost the ability to compete—what little there had been.

I ask why, but again, don't have to look far for the answers. First, that year, we left my beloved home in town (my security, my childhood romance) for an isolated new house in the country, miles from anyone and no sidewalks for bikes. Second, mother became ill.

She was mysteriously taken away—my love, my security—and we were not told why. Was she dying? We didn't know. Why did she too begin to reject me? I sent up a flare for help; I don't remember receiving any.

At home, we were victims of dad's tension. I remember my first feelings of revolt toward my father when we were made to pick up endless sticks and pinecones in the new yard while Mother was in the hospital, and thereafter. I remember commenting to Jack how unfairly we were being treated and how poor an example of fatherly love we were receiving. And the daily drinking worsened about that time. After that, I don't remember ever having an anxiety-free relationship with him.

I still resent the drinking. It was (and is) still very selfish. When he did it (and this was every time I had an opportunity to spend time with him—otherwise the father and son growth time) I tuned him out, cast him aside. He became stupid, unappealing, indecisive, someone I wasn't proud of. And, of course, Mother's aversion to alcohol was significant and pronounced with her family's propensity for alcoholism.

Today, I hear the ice hit the bar glass and I get angry. The sound spells the abrupt and undesired ending of any quality time we might have shared. The best example is his choosing to have four drinks at lunch the day he drove to visit me and lend his support after learning of my illness. His heart was in the right place. He is a genuinely loving man and has felt terribly unloved and rejected by me. He triggered my negative responses to him and the hurt then came full circle but he spoiled his effect again, by squashing that flame of myself that so desperately seeks intimacy with my father.

It is no wonder, then, that I look at someone like Joe and desire to be like him, desire to be him, with all that I am not. He, his completeness, fills a vacuum, makes me complete. Yet, I am smart enough to know I neither need nor can have him. What I need is the assurance of self-acceptance. I need the corroboration of a male figure in my life to accept me as I am and to love me as I am. Here lies the root of the great conflict.

The things Joe and others are are the things I desire to be. Free from conflicts and anxieties, confident not only in strengths but in weaknesses, and assured, in any situation, of self-acceptance and of God's acceptance.

The disapproval of myself was learned; I imitated it and it has been clinging to me like a second skin.

This is the story of a sharp, capable, successful young man, who doesn't feel that way. What happened? How does Roy build a positive self-esteem out of the shambles presented above?

Dr. Joseph Aldrich described Roy's plight well. "It's as though we come into life carrying a bucket in each hand. Emblazoned on one bucket is a big plus sign. Into this bucket go all the positive bits of information we receive about ourselves. The other bucket holds the negatives, the putdowns, the sarcastic remarks, the cruel and insensitive comments which focus on our weaknesses and inadequacies.

"If the negative is not balanced—indeed overweighed—by an overwhelming bucket of positives, our personal sense of worth, our self-image, is in danger of becoming warped and distorted. Sometimes we become so buried under negatives that we put a lid on the positive bucket and are no longer capable of receiving and accepting a genuinely positive compliment."

If we tell Roy to start thinking positively about himself, or begin to change behavior and he'll feel better, it would be like asking a toddler to run a Marathon.

No one has a perfectly positive self-image. Roy's is an extreme case. If one puts together all the concepts shared in this book thus far, we might watch Roy grow.

We begin by examining the negative bucket mentioned by Aldrich. Where did all these negative voices originate? Parents, brothers and sisters, school mates, teachers, religious leaders, relatives, all have an impact on our self-perception.

"I hear you, Dr. Burwick," a young mother piped up in a counseling session. "God revealed to me that I could not become the new creation he intended me to be without giving up the old self, or the old self-image of who I thought I was or should be. This seems easy, but it's really not. In order to do this I had to know the very root of that self-image. God is faithful and he began to show me.

"My image went back very far to my childhood. The expectations my father had for me were planted deep. He had wanted me to be someone I was not created to be. Trying to live up to those expectations had created a negative self-image. It was truly ugly and black."

Nell went on to share how one night she had had to wrestle through with God. In prayer, God revealed to her how she had to let go of the false and destructive image of herself she was carrying.

Whether her dad meant it or not, his rejection of her had distorted her identity. She had to be willing to let go of a negative identity which then would give her "no identity" before she could build positive identity.

Nell reported that by 4 A.M. she was so weary of the battle, that it was as though "God pulled the negative self-image from me."

She was challenged to say "no" to any further negative thoughts about herself.

Part of her wrestling that night dealt with forgiveness. She had to forgive her father for his rejection. Forgiveness doesn't come easy. But positive self-image cannot be built if any resentment is being harbored.

Roy and Nell have given us examples of subtle rejection. Their fathers were not the cruel, verbally and physically abusive parents. This obvious rejection is easier to see and often easier to forgive. Roy and Nell had to see that not living up to a parent's expectation is devastating. It can not be excused or rationalized, only forgiven and replaced.

Reading Charles Solomon's *Ins and Out of Rejection* has been helpful for many of my clients to see more clearly the roots of their negative self-esteem.

Reading my book *Anger: Defusing the Bomb* then helps them see the destruction of resulting resentment and how to work through it by forgiving.

As clients like Roy and Nell leave my office after the first visit, they're usually armed with an assignment that looks like this:

1. Pray Psalm 139:23-24, seeking not deep self-examination, but the Holy Spirit's revelation. "Show me, God, what is going on inside of me, my hurts, resentments, and guilts."
2. Write what surfaces in the form of a negative autobiography, in five-year segments (0-5, 6-10, 11-15, etc.).
3. Hurts, resentments, and guilts will have to be resolved. Reading the *Anger* book will be helpful.

   This part of the assignment is dealing with the negative bucket. I like to begin to fill the positive bucket at the same time.
4. Read Romans 6—8 daily. Chapter 6 describes the ideal self-image. Chapter 7 declares it impossible to live. Chapter 8 shows that it can be lived only in the power of God's Spirit. Thirty days of Romans 6—8 has made a deep impression on many.
5. Eat a well-balanced diet. Omit most sugar and salt.
6. Begin an exercise program (adaptable to each individual), walking, jogging, swimming, or other sports.

Eating right and getting consistent, sensible exercise helps you feel better about yourself.

7. Ask yourself who needs your love? Reach out to make someone else's life better.

People leave the office that first day with different attitudes. Some are excited and dig into the project assigned them. God is a rewarder of those who diligently seek him. They return in a week or two with radiant faces, on their road to becoming all that God has created them to be. A breakthrough can be quick, but growth takes the rest of our lives. We must be patient.

Others leave the office that first day with the same determination. However, as the hurts and hates are met, the struggle begins. They return to the office with insights, but not victory.

"I don't want to forgive my father." Excusing or rationalizing obstructs forgiveness and keeps some back from wholeness.

One lady said: "As I wrote my autobiography it was like venom flowing through my fingers. Writing was freeing, but I'm not ready to resolve it."

Some leave the counseling office not wanting to accept personal responsibility for changes they need to make. They continue to blame others and either do not come back or they come back with all sorts of reasons why they would be all right if the other person would just change.

For a person desiring wholeness and godliness, suggested reading includes David C. Needham's *Birthright* (Portland, OR: Multnomah, 1979), Miles J. Stanford's *Green Letters* (Grand Rapids: Zondervan, 1975), and Charles Solomon's *Handbook to Happiness* (Wheaton, IL: Tyndale House, 1971).

The following counseling sessions I have with such clients center around clarification of insights learned and checking balances. Truth out of balance leads to downfall.

Great insights not put into action lead to a lazy "rocking chair" religion. Action without knowing God and self leads to a works-oriented religion, ending in burnout.

Roy took the first assignment seriously. He even drove back to his boyhood home to relive memories. He produced a long list of people who had hurt him. It became easy to see his great hostility to his father, whom he could never satisfy.

That first week, he also dug into the reading project. His evaluation of the week: "I feel better and work is going much better."

To deeply forgive his father seemed one of Roy's major hurdles. Writing more feelings about his father was suggested for the next assignment. Augsburger's *Freedom of Forgiveness* was recommended reading for the week.

Some feel that to go back to the past means that we blame others for our problems and dwell too much on the past. One pastor's wife told me, "I'll never go back into my memories and dig up that muck. It's too devastating."

Our intention should not be to blame but to look squarely at reality. "This hurt. That was rejection, etc." The focus then is "What is my reaction to reality?"

The reaction is usually resentment. Until we clearly see these resentments and resolve them, there will be a contaminated self-image.

Our self-image is formed or reformed as we react to tough times and rejections. What we finally become is up to us. We can be positive or negative, bitter or forgiving, sweet or sour, as we choose. What *we become is our responsibility*.

At Roy's next appointment he reported, "I'm doing quite well. I'm not as ambitious about resolving my bitterness, but I'm working at it. My positive bucket is beginning to fill. When I feel inferior, I'm beginning to remind myself what Scripture says about me. My adequacy is in Christ. He is my Resource.

"When talking with Joe, my sexual feelings were not quite as confusing," he continued. "Before I didn't allow myself to feel any sexual feelings to Joe, though I knew there was a haunting, sexual figure within, wanting to leap out and be satisfied. I'm beginning to be more honest with myself because I know I have God's resources to straighten out my tangled life."

Along with writing, study, and mental reprogramming, Roy was advised to build the manhood area of his life. Physical exercise and tennis were begun.

"I bombed out," Roy reported at his next visit, and he handed me the writing that began this chapter.

"The doctors changed my medication. That had something to do with it. However, this weekend, I let those past hurts and present confusions overwhelm me. I wallowed in self-pity and mentally beat myself and others. I didn't even think of reprogramming my mind with Scripture."

This is a natural happening in a person's growth experience. Roy had either not been as diligent about his study time, consequently forgot more quickly who he was in Christ, or, he allowed some seeds of negative thought to take root. Instead of being resolved, they grew into the overwhelming self-pity and depression he experienced, as described at the beginning of his counseling.

As Roy saw what was happening, he renewed his challenge to allow God to continue his work in him. Freedom and wholeness developed.

Building positive self-esteem involves many factors, but basically it is cleaning out the old, negative information and behavior and rebuilding a new superstructure.

One of my clients, hospitalized for depression, wrote a parable regarding her self-esteem building experience.

"Looking from my hospital window, I could see workmen building a new wing of the hospital. There were truckloads of rubbish and trash around the site and only two workmen and two wheelbarrows to move it all.

"The little bit they could move in a wheelbarrow didn't seem to make a dent in the trash pile, but they continued working, slowly and deliberately loading the wheelbarrows with as much as they could carry, and carrying it away to the dump.

"Meanwhile, two other workers were busy putting steel support beams in place. One man operated the crane while the other man secured them in place. The man on the beams would signal to the crane operator to lift a beam with the crane and lower it into place. It took the workman quite some time to get the beam in place, but after he had worked on one or two, he seemed to find it to be much easier, and worked much more quickly. The support beam was too heavy for even the two men. They needed the crane, which had a power beyond themselves to lift it. But one man was needed to direct the crane and one man was needed to secure it in place.

"The other two workers were still working slowly and deliberately to remove the trash.

"The work may be slow and difficult, but once built, the building will be on a firm foundation—which will withstand many storms and stresses."

PERSONAL APPLICATION

How can we view ourselves in a much more positive way?

First, look in the mirror.

How is our appearance? What does the mirror say back to us? Are we clean, neat, dressed in a manner that doesn't degrade us?

How is our muscle tone? Are we exercising consistently? Do we need to lose or gain some weight? For women, is the makeup too sparse or too heavy?

If some changes are necessary, do we want positive self-esteem badly enough to discipline ourselves to carry through in a program of change?

What is the record of our achievements? Are we living up to our capabilities?

It is easy for us to expect someone else to take care of us. Lack of productivity, idleness, too much TV absorption, "sports-aholism," all hack away at positive self-esteem.

The security of a paycheck keeps some people working at less than challenging positions, encouraging less than an adequate self-image. There is a place for risk-taking. We might pray, "Lord, do I need to stay at this position for more personal growth, or am I ready to take a risk and accept something more challenging?"

What are we reading and watching? We become like the books we read, the TV we watch, and the people with whom we associate. Are our relationships with people such that build up or tear down our self-esteem?

Are we reading positive, uplifting material, or is much of our reading the opposite: newspaper (mostly negative), secular magazines (stimulating lust and greed), novels (escapism)? I'm not saying these materials should not be read, but a steady diet could contaminate positive attitudes about oneself.

Television, in addition to presenting a shallow, pleasure-seeking, self-centered life-style, has a hypnotic effect that is a demotivator. One might question the worth of much more than a couple of hours of television per week.

People who have a positive outlook on life, and who are encouraging and stimulating, and inspirational, positive, instructive reading material all help us to build a positive perspective on ourselves.

When I was involved with basketball camps, one of the motivational questions we would ask the campers daily was, "How's your PMA?"

They would shout back with gusto, "Boy, am I enthusiastic."

Bringing negative thoughts into captivity and replacing them with *p*ositive *m*ental *a*ttitude is certainly a must for the person growing in positive self-esteem. As we get our focus off circumstances and onto our resources in Christ, positive thinking is a natural by-product for many.

However, there are those who have lived with negative attitudes for so long that positive thinking must be a conscious effort daily. When applied consistently over a period of years, attitude changes and the rewards are great.

Looking sharp, achieving much, surrounding ourselves with good people and books, thinking positive, all help us to think more highly of ourselves. However, there are two problems from this.

1. What happens to self-esteem if it has been solely determined by looks, achievement, relationships? An accident of some kind could wipe out all three of these.

2. Sometimes there are such great inferiority feelings that the suggestions we have mentioned don't make a dent in negative self-esteem.

We must do well, look well, be with good people. All these help, but the ultimate in self-perception is found when we see who we are in relationship to God.

IDENTITY BASED UPON RELATIONSHIP WITH GOD

There are more than four billion people on earth, a planet which is but a particle within its galaxy. There are thousands of galaxies, millions of stars that are billions of light years apart. All of this is God's footstool. Yet, he is interested in me.

Since I am a Christian, God is *my* Father, and his eye is never off of me (Psalm 139). There is no moment when his care for me falters (Isaiah 41:10). He promises to work all things to my good (Romans 8:28).

How well do you and I know him? Do we spend time with him in prayer and study to know him? Are we learning more deeply the resources he has provided as we dig deep into Scripture?

Forget about moving toward the ultimate in positive self-esteem if there is not the consistent time spent daily alone with God.

"But how do I spend that time with him? What do I do?" you may ask.

There are many ways to study the Bible. One method has helped me know God better. I begin in Genesis and read rapidly through the Bible with pen and paper in hand. I divide the paper into two categories, God's blessing and care and God's judgment and punishment. As I read the Bible through, I write under the appropriate column the Scriptures that apply.

As the Scripture is read, meditated upon, and internalized, the impact is clear. God's care and blessing mean I'm significant. His discipline builds in me a sense of security. This God of whom we are speaking is *my* Father. He is El Shaddai, "The God who is more than enough" . . . my Father.

IDENTITY BASED UPON CHRIST

Not only is God my Father, which makes me significant, but his Son Jesus dwells in me through the Holy Spirit, and that blows the top off negative self-esteem.

I get a greater, clearer glimpse of who I really am as I meditate daily on Scriptures such as:

Christ in your hearts is your only hope of glory (Colossians 1:27).

This is my work, and I can do it only because Christ's mighty energy is at work within me (Colossians 1:29).

And now just as you trusted Christ to save you, trust him, too, for each day's problems; live in vital union with him. Let your roots grow down into him and draw up nourishment from him. See that you go on growing in the Lord, and become strong and vigorous in the truth you were taught. Let your lives overflow with joy and thanksgiving for all he has done (Colossians 2:6, 7).

For in Christ there is all of God in a human body; so you have everything when you have Christ, and you are filled with God through your union with Christ (Colossians 2:9).

For in baptism you see how your old, evil nature died with him and was buried with him; and then you came up out of death with him into a new life because you trusted the Word of the mighty God who raised Christ from the dead (Colossians 2:12).

Since you became alive again, so to speak, when Christ arose from the dead, now set your sights on the rich treasures and joys of heaven where he sits beside God in the place of honor and power. Let heaven fill your thoughts; don't spend your time worrying about things down here (Colossians 3:1, 2).

When someone becomes a Christian he becomes a brand new person inside. He is not the same any more. A new life has begun. . . . For God took the sinless Christ and poured into him our sins. Then, in exchange, he poured God's goodness into us! (2 Corinthians 5:17, 21).

Upon receiving Christ, I am a new creation. The dynamics of that will take me the rest of my life to understand. Even then, I

SELF-ESTEEM: YOU'RE BETTER THAN YOU THINK

won't understand fully. However, as I set aside time alone with God daily, to study new-creation concepts, the picture I have of myself becomes more positive.

I realize the resources I have, so I can reach out to others more, giving and sharing, with no expectations of it being returned. Loving others in this manner also builds positive self-esteem immensely.

In summary, we should try to look good, work hard, associate with uplifting people, bring negative thoughts into captivity, think positively, read positive material, and watch very little TV. We should include in our balanced living fun, recreation, and exercise. A well-balanced diet is of utmost importance.

Accept yourself and others as in the process of working through flaws. If you tend to be critical, don't! Set aside perfectionism. Set realistic goals.

Study Scriptures daily to know better your Father, and who you really are in Christ. Demonstrate love in action.

I have considered it a privilege to share with you readers what I believe are God-given concepts. As this book is laid aside I pray that the contents will not be.

In closing, I would hope each of you readers would join me in this prayer:

"Father, stimulate our appetites for the discipline necessary to know you better, to yield to you, to know who we are in Christ so that we may share this knowledge with the world around us. Teach us more clearly about yourself, who we are because of you, and the incredibly great power available to us because of your work within us. Father, we love you. Amen."